W9-BXU-271

Winning Basketball Drills and Fundamentals

Jerry Tarkanian

*University of Nevada
at Las Vegas*

William E. Warren

*Lyons High School
Lyons, Georgia*

Allyn and Bacon, Inc.

Boston   London   Sydney   Toronto

FERNALD LIBRARY
COLBY-SAWYER COLLEGE
NEW LONDON, N.H. 03257

For Lois,

Jodie, Pam, Danny, and George;

and

Louise, George, Sr., and Wendi

GV
885.35
.T37
1983

10/83 Newcombe 24.20

Copyright © 1983 by Allyn and Bacon, Inc., 7 Wells
Avenue, Newton, Massachusetts 02159. All rights
reserved. No part of the material protected by this
copyright notice may be reproduced or utilized in any
form or by any means, electronic or mechanical,
including photocopying, recording or by any information
storage and retrieval system, without written
permission from the copyright owner.

Library of Congress Cataloging in Publication Data

Tarkanian, Jerry, 1930–
  Winning basketball drills and fundamentals.

  1. Basketball—Training. 2. Basketball—
Coaching.
I. Warren, William E., 1941–   II. Title.
GV885.35.T37 1983   796.32'3'077   82-22672
ISBN 0-205-07817-6

Printed in the United States of America

10 9 8 7 6 5 4 3 2 1 87 86 85 84 83 82

Contents

Preface

This book provides practicing coaches with step-by-step help in teaching their players to understand and master the fundamental skills of basketball. It is divided into three parts. Part I offers a comprehensive and in-depth discussion of the fundamental skills themselves. Part II provides a systematic sequence of drills covering individual to three-man skills. Part III presents drills for developing the basic skills of team play.

Coaches do not operate in a vacuum, independent of the collected wisdom and knowledge of other coaches. We are, necessarily, borrowers and lenders (and, hopefully, contributors) in the marketplace of coaching techniques, methods, tactics, and strategy. As King Solomon observed more than 2,500 years ago, there is nothing new under the sun, and so it is today. The drills and fundamental skills in this book are not new except in the sense that they have been absorbed by us over two decades of coaching and adapted to meet our needs and the requirements of our coaching philosophy. And so it is (or will be) with you. There are no secrets in basketball except those that you are able to appropriate for yourself from among the thousands of drills and approaches to coaching formulated by coaches over the years. The real challenge lies in making these secrets work.

In formulating our philosophy of how the game should be played, we have indebted ourselves over the years to a multitude of people, including players, other coaches, and assistant coaches. Our indebtedness is unlike that of one coach who remarked, "I owe everything I know about basketball to my players. If they hadn't been so lousy, I'd never have learned anything about basketball." No, we subscribe to the belief that *the successful coach learns from everyone he meets in coaching.* Coaching is dealing with people and patterns and attempting to find compatible relationships that bring out the best in each. We have learned much from the players we've coached and from the coaches we've known or worked with. Their contributions to both this book and our earlier book, *Winning Basketball Systems*, (Boston: Allyn and Bacon, 1981) have been considerable.

In particular, we wish to acknowledge the contributions of Ivan Duncan, my assistant coach at Long Beach State and the University of Nevada at Las Vegas (UNLV) for several years, for his part in formulating the zone defensive drills in Chapter 17. Also, we want to express our gratitude to Athletic Director Grace James and Coach Scotty Perkins of South Georgia College for providing the facility for the indoor photographs in this book and in *Winning Basketball Systems*. Talbot Lovering was outstanding, as usual, in his capacity as photographer, as was Greg Cava in taking the photographs at *UNLV*. In addition, we thank Bobby Bell, Dwayne Beasley, Billy Joe Woods, Freddy Howard, and others who contributed their time and talents to the photograph sessions.

Finally, we are grateful to Louise Warren, who somehow found time between teaching and household responsibilities to type the entire manuscript three times in the course of preparing it for publication.

Introduction

Basketball is a game of habits. The importance of spending time developing sound fundamental habits cannot be emphasized enough. To develop sound playing habits, a basketball player must have a thorough working knowledge of the fundamentals of the game—not just a general understanding but also a mastery of their detail. Individual fundamentals are synonymous with sound habits of team play. There is only one way to develop these fundamentals—through rigorous repetitive work and daily practice sessions. Mastery of fundamental skills is the first principle of winning basketball.

The fundamental skills of basketball—passing, shooting, rebounding, dribbling, and offensive and defensive stance and footwork—provide the basis for individual development and improvement. Players may excel in certain aspects of the game because of their natural talents (such as relying on their vertical jumping ability or height in rebounding rather than learning to position themselves so as to block their opponents away from the boards; still, attention to fundamentals is never wasted. However talented players are as a result of their speed, quickness, coordination, or peripheral vision, for example, they cannot help but improve their performance by practicing fundamentals.

All basketball reduces to fundamentals. The tall player must be mobile enough to free himself to receive the ball when facing defensive pressure inside and strong enough defensively not to commit fouls every time the opponents' big man gets the ball. Smaller men, however quick, must be able to play position defense or else surrender offensive numerical superiority to the opponents whenever opposing ballhandlers penetrate beyond them. Certainly, natural talent is a factor in a player's ability to master the skills of basketball. One can't argue with Bobby Knight's comment that you can teach a kid to shoot or play defense, but you can't teach him to be 7 feet tall. Yet we as coaches sometimes forget our responsibility to help players reach their potential through drill and practice work with fundamentals.

Every movement in basketball except running is artificial and unnatural to a certain extent. All movements, from the seemingly simple act of pivoting to the awkwardness of shooting a jump shot for the first time, must be learned with the same kind of diligent training and practice that accompanies studying ballet. It is important to be exact in teaching fundamental skills. Often some seemingly insignificant factor determines whether the skill is learned properly or not—and, once learned incorrectly, a skill must be "unlearned" before it can be replaced by proper techniques.

The coach's role and responsibility are to provide players with a planned program of drills and instruction that will enable them to master the fundamental skills necessary to reach their potential in basketball. Regardless of how many naturally talented players are on the team, the coach should emphasize the improvement of fundamental skills at every opportunity. Players should also be encouraged to work individually in the off-season. Many players develop their skills after basketball season is over and by the start of the next season are much better players.

The coaching task consists primarily of teaching skills and eliminating mistakes. Though it is nice to have a superstar or two, teams can learn to win consistently with average players executing average skills by following the simple practice of *eliminating mistakes* and *improving skills*. The coach is the person responsible for identifying areas of individual and team weaknesses and for taking steps to improve performance in these areas. You won't teach skills through scrimmaging unless you stop the scrimmage to correct mistakes or arrange your scrimmages so that certain game-related areas of individual or team weaknesses receive intensive practice beyond that found in nonstop full-court scrimmaging. You won't correct players' mistakes merely by identifying them in the course of scrimmaging unless you also provide opportunities to practice those skills through repetition and drill.

This is not to say, however, that scrimmaging is inherently wrong or that drills by themselves will produce championship teams. Drills are only one aspect of a team's overall preparation for basketball, albeit an important one. Unlike the pursuit of individual and team goals that sometimes becomes confused in scrimmaging, engaging in drills is always specific and thus keeps the players' attention focused where it should be.

Since they are sometimes used interchangeably, the terms *scrimmaging* and *drilling* should be defined. In scrimmages, teams perform under circumstances more or less identical to those found in games. The scrimmaging may be either full or half court in nature, but little attention is paid to correcting mistakes through constant repetition of a given skill.

In contrast, while drills may be performed full or half court and for a long or short time, emphasis is always placed upon *repetition of given skills in brief segments.* For example, a coach may drill players in transition basketball by playing a certain half-court defense, (man-to-man or zone defense) and by fast breaking every time the defensive team steals the ball or claims a rebound. Used as a drill, this exercise stops whenever the fast-breaking team fails to score on the fast break. The players then return to their same positions, with the ball returned to the offensive team to begin the drill again.* (Otherwise, when the fast-breaking team failed to score and set up in its half-court offense, it would have been practicing skills other than those directly related to transition.)

In summary, although drills and scrimmaging are similar, they are not identical and should not be confused as such. Both have their proper place in the preparation of basketball players and teams. If your team doesn't need drills, don't use them; however if full-court scrimmages are a way of life for your team, don't expect your players to pick up new skills or correct their mistakes easily without drills.

We have included not only drills we are using now at UNLV, but also zone defensive drills and techniques developed during my years at Riverside City College, Pasadena City College, and Long Beach State as well as a broad variety of conditioning, team, and individual drills of varying difficulty. Some of the drills are extremely basic, but we have attempted to provide drills to meet the needs of players on varying skills and experiential levels.

* This technique is known as *controlled scrimmaging.* It combines aspects of both drilling and scrimmaging.

Fundamental Skills

I

Offensive Stance
and Footwork

Before discussing the footwork patterns required of moving players, we should note that proper footwork begins with a player's stance. A player's stance will help determine the speed (and body control) with which he can begin moving from a stationary position or vice versa.

The basic offensive stance of a player with the ball is identical to that of the basic defensive stance, with the single exception that the player has the ball in his hands. This position (Figure 1–1) is commonly known as the *triple-threat* position, since a player who has not used up his dribble may either pass, shoot, or dribble from that stance. (If, for example, the player is standing erect and holding the ball overhead (Figure 1–2), he is restricted to using an overhead pass or bringing the ball down low to begin dribbling. This kind of alteration is unnecessary if the player holds the ball in the low, balanced triple-threat position.

Circumstances may dictate, however, that the player assume a stance such as the erect stance with the ball overhead or with the ball held low and body turned away from the defender in order to protect the ball (Figure 1–3). Nevertheless, players must learn to assume the triple-threat position if they are to derive the benefits to be gained from its usage.

3

Figure 1–1 Triple-Threat
Stance

Figure 1–2 Erect Stance (Ball
Overhead)

4

Figure 1–3   Protected Stance

POST POSITIONING

When posting inside, a player should make his body as broad as possible in order to give the passer as big a target as possible and at the same time force his defender to the side and away from him (Figure 1–4). The most common mistakes made by inexperienced post players are (1) standing erect with hands at the side, a position that permits the defender to reach all the way across the post man's body to deny passes, and (2) failing to maintain a positioning advantage when it arises.

Figure 1–4   Stance at Low Post

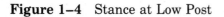

Figure 1–5 Combating Inside-Out Defensive Coverage at Low Post (*a*)

As far as this second mistake is concerned, it is unreasonable to expect the defender to surrender the offensive positioning advantage without fighting to retain defensive control of the post position. If, then, the low-post defender is guarding "from the inside out" (Figure 1–5), he will move toward the free-throw line in sliding around to overguard or front his man. The offensive post man who

Figure 1–6 Combating Inside-Out Defensive Coverage at Low Post (*b*)

Figure 1–7 Combating Inside-Out Defensive Coverage at Low Post (*c*)

wants to maintain or improve his advantage will not let the defender step up to overguard or front him but will move toward the free-throw line with the defender, thus making it harder for the defender to get around him into position to deny the pass. In maintaining an erect stance, the post player should keep his hands and arms extended upward and outward, even while moving, in order to keep the defender away from him. If the defender fails to adjust to this situation, he will find himself (and in all likelihood, his team as well) vulnerable to a lob pass inside to the post man, cutting back toward the basket. (See Figures 1–5, 1–6, and 1–7.)

Of course, if the defender's post positioning is "from the outside in" (Figures 1–8, 1–9, and 1–10), the offensive post man will again move with his man to keep him outside and away from himself, with the same end result, the cut to the basket and lob pass for the layup. Though this technique is far less common than the *inside-out* technique, particularly in zone defense, we use *outside-in* low-post coverage in our pressure man-to-man defense, relying on pressure on the ball to deny the pass to the post man reversing to the basket.

Figure 1–8 Combating Outside-In Defensive Coverage at Low Post (*a*)

Figure 1–9 Combating Outside-In Defensive Coverage at Low Post (*b*)

Figure 1–10 Combating
Outside-In Defensive Coverage at
Low Post (*c*)

FOOTWORK

One of the most neglected phases of basketball instruction from both
offensive and defensive standpoints is the proper use of footwork.
Coaches often overlook this part of the game and consequently delay
to a certain extent their players' individual improvement. A great
deal of time early in the season should be spent teaching proper
footwork, turns, pivots, fakes, change-of-direction running, body
balance, and running under control.

Proper body balance requires that the player's weight be distributed evenly. The knees must be flexed, with the center of gravity
carried on an imaginary line through the hips. The feet should be
spread but only comfortably so (except in the defensive stance). The
arms should be positioned away from the body, but the elbows should
still be in close enough so that one can move his hands quickly in
either direction.

To be effective in basketball, players generally must establish
a low base of operation. The flexed-knee position and a low center
of gravity ensure rapid movement in all directions and improve the
player's ability to jump quickly. Players should, at all times on the
court and whether on offense or defense, maintain a flexed-knee

stance. Every part of basketball, every phase of the game, is initiated from the flexed-knee position. Special drills should be used to help an individual develop proper body balance, with particular emphasis placed upon the tall player in using these drills. Many of these large players will develop practically overnight when these footwork drills are mastered.

Change of Direction

Every player eventually discovers the importance of being able to fake in one direction and then cut in a different direction. The move itself is easy to execute but difficult to do effectively. Some players have a tendency to jump into the move rather than stride into it.

To be effective, the first step, or fake step, must mean something to the defensive man. If the step is too short, the defensive man will not react. If it is too long, it will be too hard for the player to make the second step. If a player wants to fake left and go right, the first step with the left foot should be a strong step carrying most of the weight on the inside and on the ball of the foot. The left foot should point in slightly to help pushing out with the right foot in the other direction. To accentuate the fake, the head, eyes, and shoulders should be shifted to the left.

The first step (Figure 1–11) can be classified as a good three-quarter stop. The second step (Figure 1–12), made with the right foot, should be a full step and carry as much stride as possible. The angle of cut need be only about forty-five degrees (Figure 1–13). Controlled speed is essential in making the move effective. It is

Figure 1–11 Fake-and-Cut (Without the ball) (*a*)

Figure 1–12 Fake-and-Cut
(Without the ball) (*b*)

better to go too slow than too fast, for the player to walk through
the move at first and then increase the speed as his skill is developed.
The move is effective because of its execution, not because of its
speed.

The Jump Stop

The ability to execute a jump stop is an important aspect of good
footwork. The jump stop is executed when the player takes off from
the floor while in motion, jumps forward, and plants both feet on
the floor simultaneously. He has not established his pivot foot be-

Figure 1–13 Fake-and-Cut
(Without the ball) (*c*)

cause both feet have been planted on the floor at the same time. Because both feet landed on the floor simultaneously, a reverse turn can now be made with either foot used as the pivot foot. In accomplishing the movement of squaring the feet, as his rear foot swings forward into the air, the player takes a small skip-step or hop with his other (front) foot so as to land with his feet perpendicular to the basket. From such a position he is ready to shoot, pass to a teammate, or establish *either* foot as his pivot foot. He has also minimized the possibility of traveling with the ball, since stopping on both feet tends to drastically reduce forward momentum. (See Figures 1–14 and 1–15.)

The significance of this point—establishing either foot as one's pivot foot—cannot be stressed too greatly. When a player catches the ball while running, his next foot to touch the floor is established as his pivot foot; that is, after catching the ball, he is allowed to take only one step (except when he is shooting a layup) before shooting or passing the ball. When he catches the ball while running, he cannot choose his pivot foot, and if he gets in trouble, he still must use that foot as his pivot foot.

Figure 1–14   Jump Stop (*a*)

Figure 1-15   Jump Stop (*b*)

In catching the ball with feet squared, however, he can pivot either way, and on either foot, in order to avoid trouble, since either foot may take the next step that establishes the pivot foot.

A player can use as many as four pivots after jump stopping. The proper mechanics of this move include low body weight, flexed knees, and heels positioned so that they absorb the weight as the feet are planted. If the weight is absorbed on the balls of the feet, the momentum of the stop will invariably cause a shuffle of one foot in reestablishing weight control. This will in turn establish the foot not in motion as the pivot foot and restrict potential movement to one direction instead of two. The important principle involved is the weight absorption carried on the heels as the feet contact the floor.

The Stride Stop

The running stride stop is a more natural move for players to use than the jump stop. Many years ago coaches insisted on the jump stop, but now the tendency is to develop the proper use of the stride

Figure 1–16   Stride Stop (*a*)

stop. A stride stop demands less coordination than the jump stop and is easier to execute for this reason alone.

   To execute a stride stop, the forward foot must be slapped down hard on the court with an equal distribution of weight through the foot to prevent its sliding. The rear foot moves forward to maintain balance. The forward foot that has been slapped down hard is the pivot foot. Full body control is not necessary in the stride stop, which can be executed at a higher rate of speed than the jump stop. The body must be low and the knees flexed to execute either stop properly. (See Figures 1–16 and 1–17.)

Pivots

For many years we have used four different pivots. We spend a great deal of time early in the year teaching our players to use these four

Figure 1–17   Stride Stop (*b*)

pivots, until their usage is natural and habitual. The way the player is played defensively will dictate which pivot he will use. Proper pivoting technique is achieved through repeated instruction in practice and through drills performed throughout the season.

The first pivot to be considered is the *front turn*. When a guard passes the ball to a center, for example, the center will step toward the ball and catch it, while at the same time executing a jump stop or stride stop. Upon making this stop, he will land with his inside foot as his pivot foot and bring his outside foot around into a front turn. In making this turn, the player's body weight should be equally distributed. The ball should be protected by being kept outside, and away from, the defensive man. The front turn should be made from a wide, low stance with the ball close to the body and protected from the defender's reach. (See Figures 1–18, 1–19, and 1–20.)

The second pivot to be considered is the *rear turn*. It is executed with the same pivot foot as in the front turn. In the front turn, the

Figure 1–18   Front Turn (Pivot)
(*a*)

Figure 1–19   Front Turn (Pivot)
(*b*)

Figure 1–20   Front Turn (Pivot)
(*c*)

Figure 1-21   Rear Turn (Pivot)
(*a*)

player receives the ball with his front foot forward, stops, and turns to the front. In the rear turn, he turns in the opposite direction, pivoting off his front foot, and brings his back foot to the inside to make a rear turn. This move is particularly effective if the defensive man is playing loose on a player receiving the ball, since he can close the gap between himself and his defender by making a rear turn. (See Figures 1-21 and 1-22.)

The same fundamental rules exist in the rear turn and the front turn; that is, the knees should be bent, the weight evenly distributed, and the ball protected throughout. These pivots should

Figure 1-22   Rear Turn (Pivot)
(*b*)

Figure 1–23   Outside Pivot (*a*)

Figure 1–24   Outside Pivot (*b*)

Figure 1–25   Outside Pivot (*c*)

be made only when the player has complete control of his body. In developing these skills, particular effort should be made to master these pivoting movements at a low speed. Once the pivots and the footwork are mastered, the drill can be speeded up.

The third and fourth pivots to be considered are executed by pivoting from the *outside* foot. Whereas in the front and rear turns the pivot is used off the front, or inside foot, the outside and reverse pivots are used off the back, or outside foot.

To execute the *outside pivot*, the player receives the ball in the same manner as in the front and the rear turns and then pivots on his back, or outside, foot. He then raises his front, or inside, foot and turns it toward the baseline or sideline, using the back foot as his pivot foot. The outside pivot is used if the player is being guarded closely and wants to get a little more space between himself and the opposing player. (See Figures 1–23, 1–24, and 1–25.)

The *reverse pivot* is used only when overplaying occurs. For example, if the defensive player overplays the forward in such a manner that the forward cannot receive the ball from the guard because his man is playing the passing lane, the forward advances using the same footwork as in the three previous pivots. However, this time, as he lands, he pivots immediately off his outside foot, reverses his direction, and cuts to the basket. (See Figures 1–26 and 1–27.)

Figure 1–26 Reverse Pivot (*a*)

Figure 1–27   Reverse Pivot (*b*)

Fakes and Feints

It is important that a basketball player disguise his intent if he wishes to increase his potential as an all-around performer. This disguise of intent is termed *faking*, or *feinting*. The ability to feint direction of movement is as important to the player as is the faking of a shot or pass. Faking can be accomplished by making movements with the ball, eyes, body, head, arm, or foot, or with a combination of these. The same moves may be accomplished with or without the ball.

As players increase their skills, their ability to fake well becomes more noticeable. Faking lends additional cleverness to their game with the employment of step-off moves, crossover steps, change-of-pace movements, and other advanced moves that mark the outstanding performers in the game. These moves, done without conscious reflection, are developed only through constant practice.

INDIVIDUAL OFFENSIVE MANEUVERS

Various maneuvers can help an offensive player become a more effective offensive threat once he receives the ball. To free himself for a shot, a player must first evade his defender. Proper footwork and fakes enable a player to gain an offensive advantage and develop confidence in his ability to do so. We teach our players two steps: the *hesitation step* and the *crossover step*. If a player can master these two moves, he should become an effective offensive threat, particularly when he utilizes his individual skills within the context of team skills. (We used to teach the rocker step but we abandoned it because it takes too long to execute, and we kept winding up with four players standing around watching the man with the ball.) Let's now discuss these three steps.

Rocker Step

When the ballhandler takes a step forward (faking), the defensive man usually retreats; when the player steps back to his original position, his defender normally moves back to *his* original position, too. To execute the rocker step fake, the offensive man makes the first step forward, but fakes the second step back with his head and shoulders. He then shifts his weight to his back foot and drives around his man with his forward foot as the defender leans forward. This fake, with its back-and-forth movement resembling a rocker motion, can be effective in dealing with aggressive defenders who attempt to deny both the drive and the outside shot. (See Figures 1–28, 1–29, 1–30, and 1–31.).

Figure 1–28 Rocker Step (Fake-and-Drive) (*a*)

Figure 1–29 Rocker Step (Fake-and-Drive) (*b*)

Figure 1–30   Rocker Step (Fake-and-Drive) (*c*)

Figure 1–31   Rocker Step (Fake-and-Drive) (*d*)

Hesitation Step

A good maneuver to fake the defensive man out of position for a quick jump shot or drive to the basket involves the use of the hesitation step. The first step is a half step, made with the heel contacting the floor, first in a normal walking motion (Figure 1–32). The step is made at a slow pace and without any convincing attempt to move forward. The player's weight is kept on his pivot foot, allowing him to then pick up his forward foot and step off in full stride (Figure 1–33). The step is a casual motion resulting in little reaction from the defender. The hesitation step is particularly effective when used in conjunction with the rocker step, using the latter to set up the defensive man, who then is much more easily fooled by the hesitation step.

Figure 1–32 Hesitation Step (Fake) (*a*)

Figure 1–33 Hesitation Step (Fake) (*b*)

Crossover Step

Of all the individual offensive maneuvers, the crossover step is the most difficult to execute. It demands good body balance, footwork, and rhythm. It must be accomplished as one motion. The first step is actually a *jab step*, or half step. It should be a slightly diagonal step to the side, with the player's weight on the inside ball of his foot, allowing his forward foot to push off and cross over in front of his body in the other direction. (See Figures 1–34, 1–35, and 1–36.)

Once a player has mastered these three moves—the rocker step, the hesitation step and the crossover step—he then can in-

Figure 1–34 Crossover Step (Fake) (*a*)

Figure 1–35 Crossover Step (Fake) (*b*)

Figure 1–36 Crossover Step (Fake) (*c*)

corporate other moves from this position. He can fake right, go left, fake left and go right, or combine these movements in other ways to keep his defender off balance through the proper use of footwork and head and shoulder fakes.

Screening

Although the terms *screen* and *pick* once differed slightly in their meanings, those differences have disappeared in recent years, and the words are now used interchangeably to refer to any technique whereby one or more offensive players either move into the path of a moving defensive player or between a defender and the player he is guarding for the purpose of blocking the defensive player out of the play.

There are two primary rules to be observed in screening. First, the player setting the screen cannot be moving if and when contact is made with the defender, and the screener cannot lean toward the defender or otherwise extend one or more parts of his body (for example, an arm or a leg) unnaturally in attempting to impede the defender's movement in covering his man. Second, when setting a blind screen (one that the player being screened cannot see until he turns around), the defender must be given room to turn around completely before contact occurs. Violations of these rules result in personal fouls.

Thus, a player who wishes to set a screen must set his screen far enough away from the defender to give him room to see the screen and avoid crashing into the screener. The screener's task is merely to set the screen; it is the responsibility of the player receiving the screen to take his man into the screen by cutting or faking.

Countless opportunities for screening arise in the course of any game. Among the most popular screening variations include: the *screen-and-roll, splitting the post, double screens,* and *screening away from the ball.*

In the *screen-and-roll,* the ballhandler may be either dribbling or holding the ball when a teammate moves up to set a screen on his man (Figure 1–37); as the screen is set, the ballhandler will dribble around the screen, brushing his man off on the screener (Figure 1–38). As the dribbler goes around the screen, the screener will pivot and roll to the basket, maintaining position on the player he screened in case the defenders switch and the screener's original defender picks up the dribbler (Figure 1–39).

Figure 1–37 Screen-and-Roll (*a*)

Figure 1–38 Screen-and-Roll (*b*)

Figure 1–39 Screen-and-Roll (*c*)

Although once widely used, *splitting the post* has been abandoned in recent years, primarily because of the emergence of defensive techniques such as collapsing toward the middle whenever the ball is passed inside. Still, the techniques involved in splitting the post are ideal for teaching players to brush their men off on the post man or another teammate.

In Figure 1–40, a guard has passed inside to high post (Figure 1–41) and is beginning his cut around high post. The other guard is maneuvering himself to cut immediately behind the ballhandler in his cut around high post, giving him *two* chances to brush his man off (Figure 1–42). In order to avoid having the cutters run into each other, teams usually have the player who passed inside make the first cut, with the other cutter scissoring immediately after him.

Figure 1–40   Splitting the Post

Figure 1–41   Splitting the Post

Figure 1–42 Splitting the Post

The offense can also split the post from the side of the court. The movements are the same as the first time; only the angles of the cuts are different.

Double screens, or screens in which two offensive players set screens on a single defender, sometimes have the effect of confusing the defenders as to which of them will switch to cover the player with the ball behind the screen. Double screens may be effected from

Figure 1–43 Double Screen (*a*)

Figure 1–44   Double Screen (*b*)

practically any offensive pattern; they occur regularly in many continuity patterns, such as the Wheel or Shuffle.

In Figure 1–43, player number 44 has cut behind an inside
double screen along the baseline to receive the ball. If his own
defender tries to get around the screen, he will be too late to stop
the shot (Figure 1–44). If the defender nearest the baseline switches
to cover the ball, an offensive mismatch may occur inside along the
baseline, and if the defender nearest the free throw line makes the
switch, the mismatch will arise inside the lane. In both cases,
though, forcing the defenders to switch will alter the defense's timing as well as its matchups.

Screening away from the ball is the kind of movement featured
in today's man-to-man offensive patterns. The so-called passing
game offenses rely heavily upon cuts and screens away from the
ball under the premise that players tend to relax slightly when the
player they're covering is on, or cutting to, weak side. Even when
the players remain vigilant, their attention is divided between the
opposite sides of the court, a factor that reduces their ability to
prepare to combat the screen.

2

Passing

GENERAL CONSIDERATIONS

1. There is absolutely no excuse for a basketball player not being able to make crisp, accurate passes most of the time. All he needs to improve his passing is a ball and a wall. He doesn't even need a partner. No single offensive skill associated with basketball (except, perhaps, for setting screens) is more often overlooked and more basic to the game than passing.

A player can compensate for poor shooting skills with a skillful defense, but no amount of shooting skill can compensate for an inability to pass the ball. The player who cannot pass the ball is helpless against pressing defenses, and he always runs the risk of losing the ball in pressure situations, especially if he is equally unskilled as a dribbler.

2. Keep the passes simple. Perhaps this can be better stated as *use the pass that is most likely to get to your receiver*. The most intricate, difficult pass is worthless if it can't be controlled or doesn't increase a team's chances of scoring.

We're not saying that there is no place in basketball for fancy passes. There are many cases in which simple chest passes just won't work, and in such situations the passer is justified in throwing whatever pass he thinks will reach the receiver. However, we've all seen cases where players tried behind-the-back or between-the-legs passes in such situations as three-on-none fast breaks, only to throw the ball out of bounds and fail to score. In most cases, the primary purpose of passing is to advance the ball into scoring areas, and passes that cannot be controlled should not be used. The truly outstanding passer may or may not be flashy, but he seldom has passes stolen or deflected, and he can get the ball to his teammates when they're open.

3. Throw passes the receiver can catch. Few things are more frustrating to a player than to work himself free, only to have a teammate's pass hit him on the knee or foot or to have an inexperienced teammate dribble up to him and release a hard chest pass directly at his face from point-blank range.

An experienced ballhandler will throw hard or soft passes as the occasion warrants. He can recognize his teammates' limitations in determining the speed, direction, and type of pass to be thrown.

A player is unlikely to catch a pass if he isn't expecting it. Part of the responsibility is the receiver's, of course, since he should have his hands up in preparation to receive passes, but the passer should also be aware that his goal is to deceive the opposition, not his teammates. If the receiver isn't expecting a pass, it should not be made.

In passing to a stationary teammate or to one moving straight at you, you should aim the ball at the receiver's hips. If passed to the receiver's head, or even as high as his shoulders, the ball may be fumbled because it must be adjusted before it can be passed again. Hard passes can be handled best if passed to the area of the receiver's waist.

In passing to a player moving diagonally across the floor, you may throw the ball higher, but never throw it above the shoulders. It takes considerable practice to pass accurately to running players at different distances and speeds so that the ball will reach them at the proper point for easy and quick handling. Timing is an essential element in accurate passing. Therefore, it is necessary to be able to judge the speed of the player and to determine how hard the pass should be thrown.

4. Beginning players should watch where they're passing the ball, but as their skills increase, they should consciously avoid watching the receiver. The reason for this apparent contradiction is that a player's first consideration is always to control the pass. Not until he can throw his passes with accuracy, regardless of the type of pass required, should he attempt deceptive passing. That is, only when he is confident in his basic skills in passing should a player pursue the advanced skills involved in deceptive passing.

5. Players should resist the temptation to make low-percentage passes. When a teammate is closely guarded, he is usually a poor risk as a pass receiver; thus, the ballhandler should avoid forcing passes to him. (This is a prime reason for not leaving one's feet in making passes, since you may be forced into desperation passes in order to avoid coming down with the ball.) If you can't make the pass, don't throw the ball. And don't throw crosscourt passes when you have other alternatives.

6. Passing (and dribbling) skill provides a means of equalizing shorter players with taller players. Although height can provide an advantage for a player, it is not necessary for ball-handling skill. Shorter players who have trouble passing over taller opponents can use speed and deception to maneuver opponents out of position and then can pass over, under, or around their outstretched arms. Skill in passing may be an added advantage for taller players, but it is a necessity for shorter players.

7. When a pivot player is also a good passer, he can control the tempo of the game, taking his own best shots and passing to teammates when they are open. In professional basketball, centers often lead the league in assists, or passes that lead directly to baskets.

8. Teammates always appreciate a player who will pass to them, especially when the passes lead to scores. If you dribble endlessly to set up your own shot or shoot practically every time you get your hands on the ball, your teammates will likely resent your actions. On the other hand, they will never complain that you "hog the ball" when your maneuvers and fakes set *them* up for easy baskets. When you pass the ball to a teammate in the clear, you have, at least momentarily, sacrificed your own chances of scoring and increased *his* chances of scoring—an act that leads to his appreciation of your unselfishness.

9. After passing the ball, don't just stand there—do something! You can set screens for the receiver or other teammates, break to the basket for a return pass, or simply move away from the ball in order to permit the ballhandler to work one-on-one. Practically the only thing you can do to hurt your team's efforts is to stand still and watch the game.

FERNALD LIBRARY
COLBY-SAWYER COLLEGE
NEW LONDON, N.H. 03257

Figure 2-1   Chest Pass

KINDS OF PASSES

The Chest Pass

The chest pass is to basketball what the dive play handoff is to football: the basic pass of basketball. It is versatile, easily controlled within a range of about twenty feet, and can be executed with accuracy at any speed. It is called a chest pass because the passer brings the ball with two hands to the vicinity of his chest, with his fingers covering the sides of the ball and his thumbs behind the ball, pointing inward. (Actually, the ball should be held close to the stomach, not the chest. Holding the ball high tends to eliminate the effective use of bounce passes.) The elbows should be in close to the body, and the ball should be released with a push and snap of the wrists and fingers. Follow-through with both arms completes the pass. Slight backspin is imparted by the fingers and wrists flipping the ball as it leaves the passer's hand. (See Figure 2-1.)

The chest pass may be made with one or two hands. In the two-hand form, the passer's thumbs should point toward the floor, with his palms facing the receiver after he releases the ball. Beginners are advised to step toward the person to whom they are passing, although there are many situations in which taking a step is inadvisable or impossible. In the one-hand form, the same foot as the passer's throwing arm should go forward with the throw.

Figure 2–2   Bounce Pass

The Bounce Pass

A bounce pass is a chest pass thrown in such a manner that it strikes the floor before it reaches the receiver. It is a soft, relatively safe pass, since the usual means of deflecting it is to kick at it. Bounce passes are used primarily in two situations: passing inside against zone defenses and at the end of fast breaks. A bounce pass is likely to be successful any time the defender has his hands up—for example, when a defender is waving his arms overhead to prevent a long pass downcourt or lob pass inside to the low post area. (See Figure 2–2.)

Every effort should be made to reduce the spin imparted to bounce passes. A little backspin won't seriously impair the pass, but too much backspin will cause the ball to bounce high. The passer's body should be in a balanced, crouched stance, and he should release the ball with a snap of his wrist and fingers so that the palms of the hands will be facing the floor with thumbs in.

The Lob Pass

A lob pass is a high, arcing pass usually made for the purpose of passing over a defensive player. It may be thrown from a regular chest pass position if the ballhandler is not guarded closely, but it occurs more often as a two-hand overhead pass. Because of its high arc and the amount of time the ball is free (that is, not in the possession of either team), the lob pass is considered risky in most situations.

Players should avoid making crosscourt lob passes and should use passes other than lob passes whenever the ball must be passed quickly. The possibility always exists that a defender might step between the passer and receiver to intercept or deflect the pass— especially in situations such as stalling or advancing the ball down-court against presses. When the passer intends to lob inside to a player posted low, his task is usually made more difficult by the inside defender overplaying the low post, since in this situation the passer not only must lob over his own defender but also must direct the pass to the side of his teammate away from the inside defender.

The Two-Hand Overhead Pass

The two-hand overhead pass is a highly specialized type of pass whose usage belies its difficulty. It is often used by tall players or by a receiver who has caught a high pass and wishes to make a quick return pass. This pass-return-pass sequence has become popular in recent years. We used it with a high degree of success at Long Beach State, with 6'6" guard Ed Ratleff passing to a forward, then cutting into the pivot for a return pass.

The two-hand overhead pass is difficult to defend against. The ball should be held overhead with both hands; the pass is made by flicking the wrists, with the elbows locked in a straight-arm position throughout. The pass is best executed by stepping forward with either foot and throwing the ball with a slight downward motion of the arms. The two-hand overhead pass is advantageous in that the defensive player must stand up straighter to block overhead passes, the ball can be protected rather easily, and it provides a natural way of making lob passes. Its disadvantages are that beginners have difficulty controlling the pass, that only one type of pass can be made effectively from a position above the passer's head, and that most players are unable to make long passes of this type.

The Baseball Pass

The baseball pass, so named because the throwing motion resembled that involved in throwing a baseball, is a more specialized type of pass than the two-hand overhead pass. Its chief value is that it provides a means of throwing long downcourt passes, although it is difficult to throw without putting sidespin on the ball. (Sidespin not only causes the ball to curve but tends to make it slide through the receiver's hands.)

Thrown properly, the baseball pass can be a formidable offensive weapon. A simple checkpoint to determine whether it is being thrown correctly is the position of the palm and fingers of the passer's throwing hand after releasing the ball: if the fingers point toward the intended receiver, with the palm toward the floor, the pass will have backspin—and in passing and shooting, *backspin* means *control* of the ball. On the other hand, if sidespin is evident, the passer's fingers and palm will point perpendicular to the intended line of flight. (See Figures 2–3 and 2–4.)

Figure 2–3   Baseball Pass (*a*)

Figure 2–4   Baseball Pass (*b*)

The Shovel Pass

The shovel pass is an underhand pass thrown or handed with one or both hands. These passes can be useful in situations in which (1) the ball is caught low and passed from that position, (2) the defender's hands are high, (3) the ball is transferred as teammates cross (as in splitting the post or weave patterns), or (4) extremely cautious ballhandling is indicated.

When two hands are used, the shovel pass may be thrown with backspin or no spin at all. When the ball is handed to a teammate, the passer extends the ball waist high to shoulder high, then holds it until the teammate takes it out of his hands. In weave patterns the ball should not be passed at close range but should be handed to the intended teammate.

In three-on-two fast-break situations, the shovel pass is often used as follows: the player bringing the ball down the middle catches the ball low off the dribble and strides and fakes upward with his head and shoulders as if he were going to shoot a layup. When the defender raises his hands to reject the shot, the ballhandler shovels the ball underhand to a teammate for the layup.

The Hook Pass

Although the hook pass may be used in a variety of ways, it occurs most often after rebounds as a means of clearing the ball to the sideline to start the fast break. Passing the ball in heavy traffic, particularly that found around the basket after shots are taken, always entails a certain amount of risk, a fact that explains in part why hook passes aren't used more often. Nevertheless, for starting the fast break it is faster to use a hook pass as an outlet pass than to have the rebounder dribble out of traffic before making the pass.

In making a hook pass, the ball is held in the throwing hand, waist high, with fingers spread and the ball against the wrist. The free hand and arm are turned toward the defensive man. The passer takes one step away from his man, jumps, turns in the air, makes a modified hook-shot pass to a teammate, and lands with knees bent, perhaps to swing into a sideline lane in the fast break.

Fancy Passes

Any pass that is more difficult than necessary to get the ball to the receiver may be termed *fancy*. The fancy passes—behind-the-back, between-the-legs, behind-the-neck, and trailer passes—are not necessarily harder to throw than other types of passes, although they may require a greater degree of ball control in order to be executed successfully. They are crowd pleasers, and therein lies their danger: that players might get so caught up in entertaining the fans with unnecessarily clever passes that they lose sight of their primary offensive objective, which is scoring points.

Behind-the-Back Pass. The behind-the-back pass is usually thrown off the dribble—that is, the ballhandler never actually catches the ball with both hands but catches it with one hand and flips it behind his back to a teammate in the same motion. The dribbler catches the ball off the dribble with his hand on top of the ball, gaining control as it rises, and then quickly turns the ball to a point where his hand is slightly under and to the side of the ball.

Figure 2–5 Behind-the-Back
Pass

Without interrupting the movement, he swings his hand (and the ball) across his back and then flips the ball toward the intended receiver with his wrist and fingers (Figure 2–5).

The passer's wrist and fingers guide the ball, and speed is supplied by his hand swinging across his back. Behind-the-back passes may be thrown as either straight or bounce passes, but in both cases they usually have topspin or sidespin.

Between-the-Legs Pass. Unless you have long legs and extremely good coordination and ball control, you aren't likely to make a between-the-legs pass while running. A few players can do it, but it is an extremely advanced skill. Most players who pass between their legs make such passes while sliding, not running, an action that lessens the effectiveness of the pass because the defender is permitted to slow down also.

Perhaps the best situation for passing between your legs, if you're determined to do it (though a chest, bounce, or shovel pass would get the job done more safely and easily), occurs when you are leading a three-on-two fast break. As you reach the top of the circle, you begin to slow down slightly and slide toward the outside guard, moving the ball to a position almost behind your body. If you're dribbling right handed, the ball will be back in a protected position on your right side and your left leg will be sliding forward. As your leg slides forward, your right hand swings the ball down and between your legs. If aimed properly, the ball will strike the floor somewhere beneath your body. This position should give the ball enough rebounding height to reach the area of the receiver's waist.

You'll have to be in a semicrouched position as you advance your dribble, however, because you must be prepared to make the pass as soon as the outside defender moves to guard you. If he's too far away when you make the pass, he may steal the pass and start his own fast break. The ideal situation for making this pass occurs when the outside defender overguards you to your right, trying to stop your drive, since the passing lane to your left will be wide open. (Of course, if he isn't in an overguarding position, you can still make the pass, but you might also drive on him.)

Between-the-legs passes are too risky in many cases to be effective. There are enough other, easier passes available and no reasons why good ballhandlers can't learn to use them judiciously.

Behind-the-Neck Pass. Again, opportunities for using the behind-the-neck pass are limited, but players are always interested in advanced or hazardous techniques, so here goes:

As you're coming down the middle leading a three-on-one or three-on-two fast break, the defenders, staying back to protect the basket area, give you the outside shot if you want it. (You don't want it, of course, so you drive on toward the basket.) As you near the guard, you catch the ball, take a step with your left foot, and leap into the air, turning toward your teammate on the right and extending the ball outward with both hands as if you were passing to him.

Of course, the defenders think you're going to make the pass, so they move over to their left, whereupon you bring the ball back to your body and then flip it behind your head to your teammate on the left. You have just completed a behind-the-neck pass, an act that qualifies you for making the fanciest pass of them all—the pass to a trailer—if you ever get the chance to use it!

Trailer Pass. Passing to a trailer is a rather unique situation. It requires that (1) only one guard is in position to stop the fast break, and (2) the ballhandler can dribble well enough to turn his head and check to see that a teammate is trailing him. The maneuver itself is simple; setting it up is the difficult part.

As you're dribbling toward the defender in a one-on-one fast-break situation, you glance around quickly for teammates and discover one behind you, trailing the play. Sensing an ideal situation for using a 'trailer pass, you drive hard toward the basket. The defender, who picked you up at the free-throw line, follows you (of course). When you go up to shoot the layup, extending your arms and the ball upward toward the basket, he goes up with you to block the shot and perhaps rearrange your face in the process. You knew he'd do this (if he hadn't, you'd have taken the shot yourself), so when he leaves his feet, you simply flip the ball behind your head, without looking, and your trailing teammate lays the ball in for two points.

A special person is needed to throw fancy passes, somebody willing to take a chance when he doesn't really have to—and maybe lose the game in the process! If you make the pass and your team scores, you're the crowd's darling (for the moment at least), but if you throw the ball away or otherwise fail to score, you're a bum. You wasted two easy points on the chance of "looking good" for the crowd, and you further contributed to your coach developing an ulcer and his need for a new employer.

If you're going to try the fancy passes, try them in practice until you have a reasonable chance of succeeding with them in games. Behind-the-back passers are made, not born.

COMMON MISTAKES IN PASSING

1. **Telegraphing the pass.** The easiest way to have a pass stolen is to *telegraph* it—that is, to show the defender where (or how) you're going to pass the ball. Although a good defensive player doesn't depend upon the passer's eyes as a reliable indicator of where the ball is likely to be passed, that information combined with other visual cues (such as turning toward the intended receiver) can tip off the direction of the pass and result in a steal or deflection.

Even though the temptation is great to do otherwise, the ball-handler must resist the urge to watch the receiver. Though there are numerous drills that provide practice at using peripheral vision in passing, the determining factor is the player's ability to discipline himself not to betray his movements. Much of the success of individual techniques in basketball depends upon deception. The player whose grasp of ballhandling fundamentals includes telegraphing passes isn't likely to surprise his opponents. Passers should release potential receivers with a deceptive move before passing to them.

2. **Putting too much spin on passes.** If any type of spin is to be imparted to a pass, it should be *backspin*, since the downward flip of the wrists and fingers in the two-hand chest pass produces backspin. Still, the spin should not be too severe, since a spinning

ball is harder to catch than a spinless, "dead" ball. A bounce pass thrown with spin may veer away from the receiver's hands after it bounces.

3. Throwing jump passes. A jump pass is one in which the passer leaps into the air before passing. It can be a formidable pass when used properly, but it is among the most difficult and risky of passes to master. In order to successfully execute a jump pass, the passer must force the defender to commit himself, then pass over or around him before landing. If, however, the defender does *not* commit himself or if another defender moves between the passer and receiver, the passer is likely to throw the ball away or commit a traveling violation by landing without having thrown the ball.

The jump pass is almost exclusively a two-hand pass, although it is sometimes thrown baseball style in making long passes. (The hook pass is a variation of the jump pass.)

Jump passes are sometimes effective when performed at high speed, as in beating presses, when the defender is unable to set himself up to jump and block the pass. Jump passes are likely to be consistently effective only when used by tall players who can use their height and jumping ability to get the ball above their opponents and then flip the ball quickly to a teammate. The player leaps into the air, extending his arms and the ball above his head, and then directs a hard pass to his waiting teammate. The force generated in the pass must come from the passer's wrists and fingers, however; if he throws with his arms, his follow-through will likely cause him to foul his defender.

Jump passes are seldom used as lob passes, since the primary purpose of jump passes is to get the ball to the receiver as quickly as possible. They should be avoided by all but the most experienced of passers, and even then their use should be dictated by necessity rather than whimsy. In the long run, constant use of jump passes in situations where other passes would suffice will beat you.

4. Bringing the ball high (or extending it outward from the body) before making a chest pass. Of all passing situations, possibly the most inopportune in terms of bringing the ball high occurs when a player is occupying the middle position in a three-on-two fast break. At such times the ballhandler wants as many passing options as possible. When he holds the ball at waist level in a low, balanced stance after catching it, he may either shoot or make a chest or bounce pass. Holding the ball high tends to reduce the passing options (except when used in faking situations).

Don't bring the ball high (in the vicinity of your head) *in passing unless you know exactly what you're going to do with it.* The same goes for leaving your feet!

There is, however, one situation in which you can leave your feet, bring the ball high, and still have an excellent chance of completing your pass (assuming, of course, that you have control of your body and the ball): in the two-on-one fast break.

There are two ways of making the pass in two-on-one fast-break situations, and both depend for their success upon good control of the ball and alertness and, to a lesser extent, upon faking ability. The ballhandler can pass directly off the dribble, using head, eye, and ball movements to convince the defender that he intends to shoot, not pass the ball; or he can go up with the ball off the dribble intending to shoot, but prepared to pass to his teammate if the defender moves to block his shot.

In the latter case, the defender must extend his arms upward to block the shot. If the ballhandler is prepared to pass off when the need arises, he should have little trouble in bringing the ball down slightly and passing it under the defender's extended arms to his waiting teammate. The key to success lies in the ballhandler's ability to make shooting his first priority, with passing used as a last resort. The ball should be held close to the body in order to generate greater force when needed in passing, to protect it, and to help disguise passes (both straight chest passes and bounce passes can be thrown from the elbows-extended position without leaving the ball vulnerable to stealing or deflection).

5. Passing without faking. Faking is essential in certain situations. For example, when a defender is guarding a player closely, one or both of his hands are usually at ball level. In such a position, he is likely to deflect passes or steal the ball unless the ballhandler can force him into a situation in which his hand(s) are no longer in the vicinity of the ball.

In order to be effective, a fake should look exactly like a regular pass up to the point where the ball would normally be released. It is here that the need for discipline arises, since there is a temptation to abbreviate the fake and get rid of the ball as quickly as possible. If the passer fails to convince his defender that he is going to make a certain pass from a given angle, the defender is far more likely to block the pass than he would if he were unsure how the pass was to be made.

The two most common faking sequences are (1) fake high and pass low, and (2) fake low and pass high. In the *fake-high, pass-low* sequence, the ballhandler swings the ball forward from an overhead position as if he were making a two-hand overhead pass. As the defender raises his hands to block the pass, he brings the ball down quickly and passes the ball under the defender's upraised arms— usually (but not always) executing a bounce pass. The *fake-low, pass-high* technique is the opposite of the fake-high, pass-low movement. The passer fakes the low bounce pass and, when the defender drops his hand(s) to block the pass, brings the ball up quickly and flips it by the defender's head. Since some players take* certain fakes more than others, a player should be able to execute both of these faking techniques.

6. Carelessly aiming or timing passes. The beginning-to-average player seldom aims his passes but merely throws them in the general direction of the receiver and hopes for the best.

When the receiver is stationary, he should not have to reach to catch a pass; that is, if the pass is thrown accurately, it will strike his body at some point between the waist and shoulders if he fails to catch it. These passes are more easily handled than passes to the receiver's knees or to above his head. No matter how fast the passer is traveling or how many contortions he has to go through prior to releasing the ball, his goal should always be to make his passes as easy to catch as possible. A player should never be in a hurry to make a good pass.

Ballhandlers should avoid making wild or blind passes. Don't make passes when you don't know who is going to catch the ball. You should know the exact location of your receiver and the nearest defenders before you pass the ball. Don't be the player who leaps to catch a ball going out of bounds and then throws it wildly over his head back into play only to find that he's thrown the ball to the opponents and started their fast break for them. *If you don't know where you're passing the ball or to whom you're throwing it don't make the pass!*

7. Not catching the ball. Though you can wheel around opponents with the most breathless set of moves and fakes ever seen or make passes over, around, and through opponents, all this talent will be wasted if your teammates cannot catch your passes. Catching the ball is a vital aspect of any player's total game. Catching passes is easy, but several points should be explored:

1. The receiver's fingers should be spread and pointed away from the ball, in order to avoid jammed fingers.

* *To take* a fake means to react to it.

2. The receiver should step toward, and reach out for, the ball rather than catch it near his body. Doing this cushions the impact of the ball and helps to protect it.

3. The receiver should watch the ball until it is all the way into his hands. A player should know where his teammates (and the opponents) are, and the time to determine their whereabouts is before the pass is attempted.

4. A good player goes to the pass rather than waits for it to come to him. Not all the way, of course, but he goes a step or two to help avoid stolen or deflected passes.

5. Probably the most common mistake associated with catching passes is the player's failure to gain control of the ball before beginning other movements. Of course, this does not mean that the player should stand still until he catches the ball. However, he must ensure that he *catches* the ball and *controls* it before he does anything else with it.

6. Players should practice catching the ball and moving it quickly into shooting position. Some of the best basketball players in the world have been at their best offensively when playing *without the ball*, working their way around screens for passes, and then going up for the shot without dribbling. It's a good skill to develop. Players also should learn to receive the ball and pass in one motion.

7. When you can't catch the ball with two hands, (for example, in rebounding), bring the ball to your body and place both hands on the ball as quickly as possible. Even a player with large hands can control the ball better with two hands than with one hand. The threat always exists of having the ball batted away when a player holds it with one hand.

8. If a player is having trouble getting passes (or dropping them), chances are that he is (1) not moving toward the ball to meet the pass, (2) taking his eyes off the ball, (3) not expecting the pass, or (4) not properly positioned to receive a pass. Ballhandlers are understandably reluctant to pass to a teammate moving away from them. The player who wants the ball will position himself so that passes can be made to him, and he will watch the ball constantly, expecting the passes to be attempted. No harm is done if the pass is not made, but anticipating the pass will make him a better receiver when the ball is passed to him.

   After catching the ball off the dribble, young players sometimes will stand with their elbows at their sides and the ball extended in front of them. Such a stance forces the ball either outward (toward their defender) where it can be stolen more easily or upward (toward their neck or head area) where their passing options may be diminished. The ball should be held near the body at stomach level, with the player's elbows extended to the sides only as far as necessary to protect the ball from defenders on either side.

TWO FOR THE ROAD

Before leaving the area of passing, let's discuss two passing patterns that can make beginning-to-average players look good beyond their experience: the pass-and-cut and quick return pass.

Pass-and-Cut

The pass-and-cut maneuver is basic to offensive basketball, yet many players fail to use it as effectively as they should. The player with the ball simply passes to a teammate and then breaks toward the basket or an open area for a return pass. It is a surprisingly successful maneuver, since many defensive players have the bad habit of watching the ball rather than the player they're guarding. When the defender turns his head to watch the ball, the passer cuts behind him to the basket, and even if the defender recovers, he will be out of position to defense his man.

Quick Return Pass

The maneuver described previously actually involves a form of quick return pass. However, there are other situations in which catching the pass and returning it immediately to the original passer can catch the offense unaware. In three-on-two or two-on-one fast-break situations, for example, the shooter can become the passer (or vice versa) by using quick return techniques. Success in such instances lies in the fact that, although the defender can change his defensive intentions after he has committed himself to a particular strategy, he will have difficulty changing his intentions in the middle of his movement.

Dribbling

Dribbling, an art once reserved for the "little man" in basketball, has now become a requirement for all players. Even the big men have acquired this skill of being able to bounce the ball more than once without catching it. Few would question the dribbling ability of 6'7" Rick Barry, 6'8" Julius Erving, or 6'8" Earvin Johnson— especially Johnson, who played *guard* at Michigan State before turning pro.

There was a time when a team might have only one man on the squad who was an outstanding dribbler, and all the dribbling was left to him. Today, every player on the team is expected to dribble in various parts of the game. However, there is the danger that a team can dribble too much. It is the responsibility of the coach and players to determine the relative values of dribbling and passing the ball. It is easier (and faster) to pass a ball up the floor to a teammate than to dribble it. Still, there are times when passes are not available, and dribbling is necessary.

With all the improvements in dribbling techniques over the years, one can understand why it is used more today in team offenses. In today's basketball, played at ever-increasing tempos with more fast breaking and pressing defenses than ever before, dribbling has become more important and popular.

Dribbling is used to advance the ball to the offensive end of the court, to initiate offensive motion, and to set up teammates for shots or play opportunities. As an offensive threat, it puts pressure on the defense. It also can be used to clear the ball away from the defensive boards after rebounds and to start the fast break by using a long first bounce in turning directly upcourt. Because defenses are forced to adjust to the motion of the ball, it is sometimes advantageous for the offense to employ dribbling. Opportunities for fast breaking depend upon the use of dribbling to a great extent. Dribbling can be used as a weapon in delay games or stalling situations. Most stalling situations are based upon spreading the five players out in the court and forcing the defense into one-on-one confrontations. In such cases the dribbler holds a tremendous advantage. Man-to-man pressing defenses force the offense to dribble, and a good dribbler can usually beat a pressing defense.

Dribbling is merely one way of moving the ball in basketball (the others are passing and shooting), yet many players use dribbling indiscriminately whenever they have the ball. All dribbling should be purposeful and not haphazard; that is, you should dribble only when you intend to use it to score or otherwise contribute to team objectives. Once you begin dribbling, you should continue to dribble until you have either accomplished your original purpose or changed it to something else that does not involve dribbling. Dribbling is a means to an end, not an end in itself.

GENERAL CONSIDERATIONS

1. Dribble with your right hand when going to your right and with your left hand when going to your left.

2. Always protect the ball with your body when being guarded closely while dribbling. Don't invite the defender to steal the ball unless (1) you're sure he can't get it or (2) you can drive around or away from him if he tries to get it.

3. Pass the ball away when opponents try to double team you as you dribble. If two opponents are guarding you, someone else on your team must be open.

4. Never dribble into a corner and stop unless you have a specific reason for doing so. You can be trapped in the corners more easily than in any other area on the court—even if you keep dribbling. When you pick up your dribble in the corner, you have eliminated one way of getting out of the corner.

5. Don't waste fakes. Use them to maintain your original advantage over your defender. After all, *you* know where you're going before the defender does. If you watch your defender's movements closely, you may discover you don't need to fake at all.

6. Don't try to dribble through zone defenses. You may be successful now and then, but you'll fail more often than you'll succeed. Zone defenses are designed to keep you from driving. If you try to dribble, you'll probably be double teamed.

7. Don't try movements in games that you can't do in practice. You'll probably have a difficult enough time performing the skills you *can* do without experimenting at your team's expense. (Of course, if you're an outstanding ballhandler, you can do as you like; however, if you're learning to play the game, you're best advised to rehearse your movements in practice before trying them in games.

8. Practice dribbling until you can dribble confidently with either hand. For example, if a right-handed player cannot dribble well with his left hand, the defense may force him to his left and take the ball away from him while he's dribbling with his left hand. Many players never learn to dribble well with both hands because they haven't taken the time to master dribbling with their weak hand.

BASIC DRIBBLING TECHNIQUES

In its simplest form, dribbling is merely bouncing the ball. You push it down, it comes back up. Nothing could be simpler, right? Not exactly. In order to control the ball, you need to have all five fingers touch the ball on every dribble, and you have to push the ball straight down toward the floor. If not, the ball won't bounce straight back up to your hand. The difficulties are compounded by the following: you can't push straight down and maintain ball control while you're moving (you'll leave the ball behind you); the position of your body is constantly changing in relation to the ball; sudden changes of speed or direction require equivalent changes in dribbling technique; and watching the ball while you're dribbling prevents you from watching the person guarding you. Thus it is obvious that the subtle changes required in dribbling techniques are as many and varied as the dribbling situations in basketball. The beginning player should devote much practice time to dribbling. You will never become a complete basketball player without learning to dribble.

The proper stance for dribbling requires that the dribbler bend his knees, carry his body weight low, hold his head up, and make his eyes look straight ahead. At any rate, he is *not* watching the ball as he dribbles. (He can see the ball at the lower edges of his peripheral vision without looking directly at it.) The ball is held in front and slightly to the side of his body. The dribbler should keep his elbows close to his body so he can have better control of the ball and be able to change hands rapidly while dribbling.

An occasional glance at the ball cannot be avoided, especially in pressure situations, but your goal should be to control the ball so that you can see all that is going on around you in order to react as quickly as possible to situations as they arise. Watching the ball while you're dribbling takes your attention away from everything else on the court, including the man guarding you. The best way to learn not to watch the ball while dribbling is to practice not watching it. You'll have to force your gaze away from it at first. If you start by selecting a spot or object near the ball, then one slightly farther away, then distant objects, then objects at eye level, and finally objects higher than your head, you should be able to gain control of the ball rather easily with either hand without losing awareness of court situations.

In dribbling, you spread your fingers (and thumb) and push the ball downward by flipping your wrist and fingers. Some elbow action occurs, but most of the push comes from your fingers and wrist. If you are dribbling correctly, your fingers will point toward the floor after you release the ball downward, but your forearm will point downward only slightly. As soon as the ball leaves your hand, you should cock your wrist again and spread your fingers to prepare to catch the ball as it rebounds from the floor.

The old teaching axiom "Don't let the ball touch the palms of your hands while dribbling" applies in the sense that the control you exert over the height and direction of the bounce is determined primarily by your fingers. "Fingertip control" also includes the pads of the hands (to cushion the impact between ball and fingers), although your fingers should do the actual work involved in catching the ball and guiding it on each dribble.

Remember that *catching* is associated with the dribbling motion. After pushing the ball downward, you should straighten your wrist immediately, which was fully bent after releasing the ball, and return it to its original position to prepare for the next dribble. You should not pat or slap the ball but *catch* it low with your wrist flexed and arm bent to soften its impact, allowing the force of the bounce to continue the ball's upward flight. (Actually, you are not "catching" the ball at all, since (1) your hand is on *top* of the ball, where you would need very large hands to catch the ball with one hand, and (2) catching the ball while dribbling—*palming* the ball— is a violation of the rules.) Controlling the dribble involves using the time that your hand is on top of the ball to gain control of the upward bounce and to guide the ball downward into the next dribble.

The height of your dribble also affects the amount of control you exert over the ball. A low dribble is more easily controlled than a high dribble but forces you to move more slowly. A high dribble permits faster movement but decreases the dribbler's control of the ball. When learning to dribble, players should not practice dribbling high. Their first concern is *controlling* the ball and, as previously stated, dribbling low allows more control. Therefore, beginners are not likely to show rapid improvement in their dribbling if they permit the ball to rise above their waists. (Another way of putting it is, "Dribble low and slow, high and fly," but low comes first.)

When the dribbler is challenged, he should protect the ball with his body. When he is not challenged and wants to move quickly, he should dribble high, with the ball rising to a point between his waist and shoulders in front of him. A good ballhandler can dribble at nearly top speed without losing control of the ball, almost as fast as he can run without the ball. As he runs, his longer strides will force him to push the ball out in front of him rather than straight down, and the faster he moves, the farther he will have to push the ball to keep it in front of him.

Problems arise when the ball is not dribbled straight down. The ball doesn't bounce as usual, and the dribbler's hand is often slightly ahead, or to either side, of the top of the ball as he dribbles. Acquiring skill in controlling the ball regardless of the angle of the bounce is imperative for all players.

High-Speed Dribbling

High-speed dribbling is performed in basically the same manner as other forms of dribbling, with a few exceptions. First, since the ball is not in contact with the dribbler's hand for a longer time than in drag dribbling, for example, it must be dribbled harder and with more forearm and wrist action. Second, the ball must be kept slightly in front of, and outside, the dribbler's path. The height of the dribble may vary considerably, but generally it falls within the waist-to-shoulder range.

Change-of-Pace Dribbling

Change-of-pace dribbling is used to keep defenders off balance or to get by (or away from) defenders. Hesitation moves, speeding up, or slowing down are all change-of-pace movements designed to reduce defensive control or create on offensive advantage.

The position of the ball is vital to the success of these maneuvers, which can be particularly helpful to players unable to dribble well enough with their weak hand to beat pressing defenses. When slowing down from high-speed dribbling, the dribbler must be careful to move the ball back and away from the defender, who will probably be closing on him in an attempt to control his dribble or take the ball away from him.

The Crossover Dribble

The crossover dribble, or changing from one hand to the other, is an essential dribbling skill. As the player dribbles with his right hand, for example, he plants his right foot down hard, an action that allows him to step off with the left foot in a different direction. On his next dribble he angles the ball to his left, thus allowing his left hand to catch the dribble. The left hand should contact the ball near the floor. The right hand is then extended to give protection from the defensive player who may be reaching for the ball.

The Drag Dribble

The drag dribble, also called protective or crab dribbling, is employed primarily by players who take their defender into the center position. It is used to gain a more advantageous shooting position after a player has received the ball with his back to the basket. (It is also used occasionally by players receiving close defensive pressure outside when they have no intention of driving or otherwise taking the ball to the basket, as in freezing the ball.) A player operating at a normal post position along the side of the lane may use drag dribbling to maneuver himself directly in front of the basket for a close-in shot. When drag dribbling, he slides, does not run with the ball, and places his body between the defender and the ball. He keeps the ball near his rear foot in a low, spread stance, with the ball dribbled as low as possible for added control (Figure 3–1).

Protecting the Dribble

All players should be taught protect the ball, a skill that is crucial to employ when a dribbler is moving laterally across the court and the defensive man is close to him. In such cases dribbling should be performed with the outside hand, or hand away from the defender, with one's free arm extended slightly to protect the ball. If the

Figure 3–1   Drag Dribble

dribbler is moving from the left side of the court to the right side, he should dribble with his right hand. If going from right to left, he should use his left hand. If he is dribbling down the right side of the court under defensive pressure, he should use his right hand; on the other side of the court, the left. Players should, therefore, be able to dribble with either hand.

Pivoting While Dribbling

Although pivoting can refer to any movement of the foot that establishes a pivot foot, we are using it here to mean "changing the direction of your intended dribbling path by partially or completely turning your back on your opponent at least momentarily." One example would be dribbling to your right and then turning to your left and away from your defender so as to dribble in a new direction.

The pivoting movement in dribbling is exactly like that involved in pivoting without the ball except that ball control must be maintained throughout the movement. In the course of a game a player may be required to pivot any number of times while dribbling, and every mistake can produce a turnover and/or score for the opponents.

An effective way of describing the pivoting-while-dribbling technique is to analyze the common mistakes associated with the maneuver. They include (1) pivoting on the wrong foot, (2) not pivoting fully enough, and (3) keeping the ball forward.

Pivoting on the wrong foot. The proper pivoting foot is always the foot nearest the defender. In moving to your right, you should use your *left* foot as your pivot foot. You should stop on your left foot and step backward and away from the defender, turning on your left foot until you have established a new dribbling path. In the previous example, if you pivot to your left on your *right* foot, you will (1) probably lose your balance and (2) definitely leave the ball unprotected. In pivoting on your inside foot, you protect the ball with your body as you turn—especially when you also bring the ball back to a point near your outside foot before pivoting.

Not pivoting fully. Pivoting is used to remove a player from danger, to move the ball away from an unprotected position while dribbling, or to change the direction of the dribble. Failing to pivot fully may allow the defender to recover his defensive position and cut off your newly established dribbling route.

Keeping the ball forward. This mistake refers to keeping the ball in front of you or slightly outside your body as you start to pivot. If you commit this error, it tends to be compounded by your having the ball stolen while it is in a unprotected position or your palming the ball. (As you pivot away from the defender, you will also pivot away from the ball.)

You should keep the ball slightly outside and in advance of your body when dribbling (except when you are being guarded closely). As you begin to pivot, you should bring the ball back to a point near your back (outside) foot. The ball will then be close to your other hand as you turn, and you will not have to reach back for it or carry it around your body. Players should practice pivoting at angles up to 135 degrees (or one and one-half right angles) away from their original dribbling routes.

Behind-the-Back Dribbling

Many coaches are reluctant to permit their players to dribble behind their backs because of the risk involved. Still, the ball control required to execute the maneuver makes it a worthwhile endeavor for players to practice, whether or not they use it in games. We've always believed in encouraging players to do anything that could improve their ballhandling skills.

Dribbling behind the back may be done while you are dribbling diagonally forward (the easier way) or straight ahead (the harder way) and while you are sliding (the easier way) or running (the harder way). Behind-the-back dribbling is easier when you are dribbling diagonally forward than when you are dribbling straight ahead because the angle at which the ball is brought around the body is less acute in the former case. Behind-the-back dribbling from a sliding stance is easier for the same reason and also because the ball, already in a protected position near the dribbler's rear foot as he slides, needs only to be pushed behind his back to the other side of his body to effect the switch to his other hand.

In terms of technique, there are two general styles of behind-the-back dribbling. The first, more adaptable to sliding than running, involves swinging the ball back slightly on the dribble and then catching it at the top of the dribble and pushing it across the back toward the other hand.

The second technique, which has become so popular in recent years that it is considered the standard method for dribbling behind the back, may be done from any position and while moving in any direction. In this method, the dribbler catches the ball low. As it rises, he keeps his hand on the ball while at the same time steering it around and behind his body and reaching for it with his other hand. This dribbling technique—catching the ball low on the dribble and steering it one way or another as it rises—is also evident in the spin dribble and provides much of the basis for today's improved ballhandling skills. Basketball traditionalists consider these maneuvers to violate the rules concerning *carrying the ball*; however, since referees almost never call violations in such cases, these arguments are moot.

The Spin Dribble

The spin dribble is widely used in basketball today, primarily to escape quickly from an overguarding defender but also to attack opponents in a variety of other ways. Spin dribbling is done in much the same manner as is the second method of dribbling behind the back, that is, contacting the ball low and steering it in a path behind the body as the ball rises from the floor. Instead of pushing the ball across the back, however, the dribbler stops with his pivot foot forward and reverse pivots, usually toward the middle, as he brings the ball around.

Armed with an effective spin dribble, almost anyone can be a dependable ballhandler, in terms of protecting the ball if not attacking the defense. The only problem associated with spin dribbling is that a defender coming from the dribbler's blind side to double team him as he pivots away from his man will be in perfect position to make an easy steal. Like most other dribbling maneuvers, the spin dribble should be used judiciously and for specific purposes rather than for show.

4

Shooting

Shooting is the most important fundamental offensive skill in basketball. A team that shoots well will always be in ball games. In this regard, knowing when not to shoot is just as important as knowing when to shoot. Under normal conditions, players should shoot only when they can reasonably expect to make their shots. Some teams are more disciplined than others in their shooting preferences, but shooting when little hope exists for making the shot is merely inviting the opponents to take the ball. Shooting strategy should be saved for occasions late in games when a team is behind and has to catch up quickly.

Many years ago, a team that had a field goal percentage of about .333 had an excellent chance of winning games. In recent years, however, with the advent of fast-break basketball, slam dunking, and the emergence of the jump shot, shooting has improved to the extent that team field-goal accuracy of 45 to 50 percent is not only common but expected of winning teams. National leaders in team shooting accuracy now hit about 55 percent of their shots, with individuals making as high as 65 to 70 percent of their shots for the season.

Shooting a basketball is both an art and a science. Shooting is an art form because it involves finely tuned hand-eye coordination rather than gross motor skills. For example, unlike such skills as the defensive stance and pivoting, which are relatively invariable, shooting form is highly individualistic. There is no one *correct* way of shooting a basketball, although there are certain elements of shooting form common to all good shooters that may be identified.

Shooting a basketball is also a science because it involves such mechanical processes as depth perception, velocity, angle of release, and trajectory of the ball in flight. The comic strip *Mary Worth* once featured an episode about a brilliant mathematics student who became an outstanding shooter on his basketball team because of his analysis of the scientific principles involved in shooting a basketball. Though the episode is rather far-fetched, it illustrates that an awareness of the scientific bases for good shooting can help to improve a player's shot within the limitations of his ability and time spent practicing his shooting.

THE MECHANICS OF SHOOTING

All the fundamentals of offensive basketball are interrelated. Shooting depends on good balance in executing the various shots and on the footwork that enables a player to get open for a shot. The actual release of all shots depends upon the proper finger and wrist control of the ball. The arc given to the flight of the ball depends upon individual preferences; however, most players are comfortable with a medium arc. Other players use a flat shot that looks as if it could barely clear the rim and enter the basket. Lowering the arc enables players to extend their range without increasing the force applied to the shot.

ELEMENTS OF SHOOTING ACCURACY

Everyone in basketball would like to be a good shooter and a high scorer. That not everyone turns out to be a good shooter or high scorer may be primarily the result of his failure to understand the elements involved in shooting proficiency (and, of course, the time spent practicing shooting). Although individual skills may limit a player's ultimate shooting ability, in far too many cases the player limits himself by his inattention to the details involved in shooting. We have identified nine elements of shooting accuracy.

Practice

Even without possessing what coaches consider to be "good" shooting form, a player can, through long hours of practice, become a good shooter and an effective scorer if he possesses at least minimal hand–eye coordination. In most cases, good shooters are the product of long hours on the basketball court practicing their shooting. Like practically everything else in life, shooting is a habitual thing; that is, it involves repetition of a given set of movements until those movements become an unconscious part of a player's court behavior.

A member of the Redheads, a women's professional basketball team, used to shoot and make free throws lying on her back at the free-throw line. Pete Maravich professes to be able to make eight of ten shots under the basket by spinning the ball on his finger and then bouncing it off his head. It's all a matter of practice. A person could probably *kick* the ball into the basket a fair percentage of the time if he practiced long and hard enough. (In fact, part of the Redheads' ballhandling act involves *kneeing* the ball into the basket from close range.)

A player may be a decent shooter without practicing if he is highly coordinated in the first place. However, he will never realize his potential without practicing shooting regularly. Consider the example of Rick Mount, who in high school took at least 200 jump shots at home every morning before going to school and kept detailed records of where and how many shots he made and missed. Not everyone has to follow this kind of schedule to become a better shooter, of course, but without a willingness to put in long hours of practice, a person is far less likely to become a good shooter.

In order to become a good defensive player, a person must be willing to work harder than his opponents, to adopt and maintain a low defensive stance, and generally to play with the kind of discomfort associated with defensive hustle. Yet no amount of hustle is going to make an errant shot go in. We recently saw a player who was working very hard on defense miss *thirteen* consecutive free throws in a single game. Poor shooting is perhaps indicative of many things, but it does *not* show whether a player is hustling out on the court. The hustle required to become a good shooter is manifested in the long hours spent on the court outside of practice.

Stance

Since shots can be taken from any body position, whether on the floor or in the air, there is no one identifiable "right" stance beyond the need for balance when setting oneself to take the shot. Because the triple-threat position offers the greatest balance and versatility, let's begin with it.

The triple-threat position refers to a low, balanced stance from which the ballhandler may either shoot, drive, or pass the ball.

Though it may seem incongruous to have the shooter lower his center of gravity prior to taking the shot because he has to get the ball *over* his defender, two factors make this move necessary. First, he needs the lowered stance to gather upward momentum for his jump shot; and second, he is more limited in what he can do with the ball when he is standing upright than when he is in a crouched position. The triple-threat position is just that, a stance from which the ballhandler may attack the defense in any of three ways.

Also, integral to any positioning before you take a shot is the action of squaring yourself to the basket, or turning your body so that your shoulders and torso are facing the basket. In their haste to get a shot away before it is blocked, players sometimes will receive a pass or catch the ball off the dribble while facing perpendicular to the basket and shoot without ever having squared themselves to the basket—for example, inexperienced players at the wing positions on zone offenses. Players should turn to the basket whenever they catch a pass or pick up their dribble. They may have to protect the ball as they turn to face the basket, but they still need to turn.

Grip

Proper grip is also fundamental to shooting success. The basic grip varies slightly from player to player, but certain common traits may be identified; the hands close together on the ball, fingers (and thumb) of the shooting hand spread, the shooting hand under (not behind) the ball, and the ball resting on the pads of the fingers and hand, not in the palm of the hand.

A one-hand shot is just that, a shot taken with one hand providing most of the force and direction. The other hand is applied to the ball mainly to stabilize the grip—that is, to keep the ball from falling out of the shooting hand and to make it more difficult for a defender to knock the ball out of the shooter's hand. The two hands should be fairly close together, with the thumbs two to three inches apart on the ball. The shooting hand should be under the ball, with the other hand on the side of the ball to stabilize the grip. (See Figure 4–1.)

The fingers of the shooting hand should be spread almost to maximum. To discover whether the spread is adequate, check the amount of daylight that can be seen between the ball and the shooting thumb and index finger. If more than one-half inch of daylight is showing, the shooter is placing the ball on a pedestal formed by his thumb and fingers. (At the same time, no part of the palm of

Figure 4–1 Shooting (One Hand)

the shooting hand should be touching the ball except the pads nearest the fingers and the fingertips, of course.)

When a player overshoots the basket consistently, he is using too much arm (particularly forearm) action and too little wrist action in his shot. The player should move his shooting hand farther *under* the ball in his basic grip and then use his wrists more and his arms less in releasing the ball. When a player gets his hand under the ball, the shot may be made more softly and with less force than when he catapults the ball toward the basket with his arms alone. Good shooting requires finesse, not brute force. (There are some limited exceptions to this rule, such as slam dunks, but we're talking about general rules applied to shooting, not specialized shots.) A player is unlikely to apply the kind of finesse needed in shooting a basketball through arm action alone.

The ball should rest on the pads of the fingers, thumb, and callused parts of the palm of the shooting hand. Good shooters don't necessarily hold the ball in their fingertips, but they *use* their fingertips in guiding the shot. If the ball rests in the shooter's palm, fingertip control will be reduced accordingly.

Finally, the shooter's elbows should be close to the body as the ball is held in front. Throughout the shot, the shooter's elbows should be kept fairly close together, as opposed to being extended to the sides. (This holds true for both one-hand and two-hand set and jump shots.) If the shooting elbow is extended to the side, the shooting hand will not be under the ball, and the shooter will thus shoot with either side spin or no spin at all, both of which provide less control than back spin.

Timing

Since timing for the jump shot will be discussed later, we will confine our discussion of timing at this point to the release of the ball *as the arms reach full extension.* Whether shooting a set or jump shot (or, for that matter, a layup), the player should keep the ball in his hand(s) until his arms are extended fully. Premature release of the ball will result in a jerky shot (in addition to a shot that is easier to block). In contrast, full extension of the arms prior to releasing the shot permits wrist action to impart back spin and "soften" the shot.

Release

In addition to fully extending the arms before the ball leaves the shooter's hand, two other aspects of proper release should be noted: the shooter's hands should be held high after the ball leaves his hands, and his wrists—at least, the wrist of the shooting hand—should be bent fully. A high release not only makes a shot more difficult to block but also facilitates the wrist flex that imparts back spin to the ball. (Using a high release does not necessarily mean that the shot will follow a high arcing path to the basket. It is possible to shoot with relatively low trajectory while using a high release, since *high release* refers to keeping the ball in the shooting hand until the arms are fully extended [Figure 4–2].)

Concentration

Shooting a basketball involves more than physical skill. The player hoping to "groove" his shot—that is, to establish proper shooting

Figure 4–2   Release (Free Throw)

habits through repetition—must be willing to put in long hours of practice. In addition, whether practicing shooting in games or in practice, he must be able to concentrate on his shot if he is to be a consistently good shooter. We've seen junior high school players watch the man guarding them as they shot rather than look up at the basket they were supposed to be aiming at; blow easy layups when they heard the footsteps of defensive players closing in on them from behind; and fumble passes out of bounds under the basket in their haste to shoot before they catch the ball.

In each case, the culprit is easily identifiable: inattentiveness, or loss of concentration. Although it is impossible to concentrate

100 percent in a ball game, that should be the goal each player sets for himself. Shooters in particular need to concentrate as fully as possible at the end of whatever movement frees them for a shot, since all the moves designed to break them free from their defender for an open shot are useless if they cannot make the shot. It's difficult, but certainly not impossible, to concentrate on your shot and on your target when an opponent is applying defensive pressure.

First, the truly outstanding offensive player will develop moves to free him from tight defensive pressure. Second, through practice under competitive conditions, he knows which shots to take and which to pass up. Third, when he decides to shoot, he is able to concentrate on the rim and his shot regardless of whether defensive pressure is applied. The prudent coach will use every opportunity to provide competitive drills, including shooting drills, designed to improve his players' concentration. Lapses in concentration lose games. In many cases, it is not the spectacular play that wins the game, but the normal play, or open shot taken and made, under circumstances in which other players are panicking or losing their concentration.

Confidence

Successful quarterbacks in football and high scorers in basketball share at least one common trait: confidence in their ability to generate offense. Without confidence, neither would be likely to achieve success. Good shooters expect to make every shot. Jerry West, for example, wanted the ball in pressure situations because he *knew* he could make the shot. He had total confidence in his ability to score, and as a result the pressure didn't bother him. Jerry's nickname, "Mr. Clutch," reflects his success in making the key baskets. He was, in fact proud of his ability to perform at his best in clutch situations, which in turn made him even more successful.

West was never a cocky player; he simply knew what he could do, and his confidence helped to ensure that he performed at high levels regardless of the situation. He knew he had ample moves to work himself free for shots, he knew he could make the shots once the opportunities arose, and as a result he seldom worried about the consequences of possible failure. He didn't expect to fail. All good shooters are "confidence" men.

Relaxation

A relaxed shooting style is the result of mastering everything we've talked about thus far. No matter how hard a player works for his shot, he should be relaxed enough in his release to shoot softly, applying as much finesse as necessary to make the shot. If a player has grooved his shot to the extent that he can make it consistently in practice with little or no variation in stance, grip or release, he must be able to duplicate that style under the pressure of game situations to be effective. Confidence and concentration will help a player to relax as he shoots the ball.

Shot Selection

Ours is rapidly becoming the era of the shooter in basketball. The players are getting better every year at putting the ball through the hoop, as evidenced by the present widespread occurrence of team shooting percentages above .500. Fifteen or twenty years ago, a team shooting percentage of .450 was considered exceptionally good: nowadays, a shooting percentage *under* .450 is considered poor.

Shot selection plays an important role in determining players' shooting percentages. In discussing shot selection, one must consider at least three important questions: Who decides which shots are "good" shots to take, the coach or his players? To what extent should the coach dictate which players should shoot and from where they should shoot? Should the players themselves be responsible for shot selection?

The logical answer to the first question is that both the coach and his players should know what constitutes a good shot *for them,* and their game plan should involve taking as many of those high-percentage shots from prime scoring areas as possible. If a team has a player who is capable of hitting at 65 percent clip inside, it would be unwise to adopt an offense based primarily on his outside shooting. If the team has a superlative player capable of dominating one-on-one matchups, as was the case with our Long Beach State teams with 6'6" guard Ed Ratleff, it would naturally want to create as many opportunities for such confrontations as possible. A team with small, quick players might run a continuity pattern with constant motion and plenty of screens to free players for layups or short jumpers. In the latter case, shot selection would involve looking for lay-ups or short jumpers off the pattern, while at the same time ignoring other outside shooting opportunities that arise.

Every coach has his own ideas about what constitutes a good shot. Before adopting a fast-breaking style of play, I considered good shots to be those made by our best offensive players shooting from fifteen feet or closer. I did not want any player shooting from farther out than the free-throw line. Logic dictated that a shot taken from thirty feet was harder to make than one from ten feet. My players wanted to take the open outside shots, but they knew I had little faith in their ability to make the shots. I gave them little leeway in choosing their shots. The more I grumbled, griped, and groaned about their outside shooting, the worse they shot, not only outside but inside as well. They began to share my doubts about their shooting ability and, as a result, I finally realized I was destroying the confidence of some fine shooters by severely restricting their shot selection.

In implementing an up-tempo style at UNLV I probably went overboard at first in giving the responsibility for shot selection back to the players, and as a result, the team took a lot of shots most coaches (including us) would prefer their players not take. Though our shot selection process was redefined to a certain extent to eliminate some shots that landed in the bleachers, our relatively unrestricted shooting style reinforced our players' confidence in their ability to make the shots they selected. Our shooters gained confidence that they could make their shots, and as a result our shooting percentages at UNLV are comparable to the old days at Riverside, Pasadena, and Long Beach. We're scoring a lot more, and the players love it!

What is a good shot? A good shot is any shot taken within the shooter's effective shooting range that he thinks he can make without having to alter his shooting style or the arc of the ball. It just isn't true anymore that players can't shoot effectively with a defender in their faces. If a player thinks he can make a given shot without altering his style to compensate for defensive coverage, we let him take it. His mind is free to concentrate on the shot when he doesn't have to look over at the bench to see whether the coaches approve. Our players still make some pretty outlandish shots from time to time, but every year we can see improvement in their shot selection as well as in their confidence and ability to make the shots.

KINDS OF SHOTS

The Layup

In preparing to shoot a layup, the player must first work out his stride pattern toward the basket. The right-handed shooter should plant his left foot and bring his right leg up high to allow maximum extension of his right arm in releasing the ball. To do this, the next to last step with his right foot is a long step, and his last step, the *takeout* step, must be short to ensure a *high* jump rather than a *broad* jump. (The short takeout step also eliminates the hard bounce of the ball off the backboard that a broad jumper sometimes gets.)

If the player is allowed to dribble to the basket, he will develop his stride pattern more easily. He should be instructed to dribble in from a forty-five-degree angle to the basket, since doing so gives him optimum room to use the backboard in his shot. The ball is carried up with both hands from the right side of the body. (The dribbler should not swing the ball to his left during his last two steps after catching the ball. Instead, he should reach across his body with his left hand to grasp the ball.) The ball should be aimed approximately a foot above the basket. It is not necessary to put spin on the ball; the natural spin resulting from finger release will give the ball sufficient spin.

There are two types of hand positions that can be employed when the ball is released. Which one is used is determined by the kind of shot taken. When traffic is heavy around the basket or when the shooter must protect the ball as he takes off toward the basket, he may elect to shoot a *power layup,* which is actually a jump shot taken at point-blank range (one to four feet from the basket). In a power layup, the player's shooting hand is behind the ball and his palm faces the backboard as he jumps, usually from both feet simultaneously. Power layups provide increased protection and control of the ball when defensive pressure is anticipated. (See Figure 4–3.)

Figure 4–3   Power Layup

The other kind of layup commonly encountered is the *under-hand layup*. The underhand layup is more of a finesse shot and leaves the shooter's hand more quickly than the power layup. Though a power layup might be used when a player cuts backdoor around a double screen to receive a pass under the basket in a Wheel or Shuffle cut, a player probably would prefer the quicker underhand layup if he stole the ball and dribbled the length of the court for a layup.

In shooting an underhand layup, the player catches the ball off his last dribble as usual but then turns the ball so that his shooting hand is directly *under* the ball, thus allowing the ball to roll off his fingers toward a point about a foot above the basket. His arms should be extended full length either outward or upward (pref-

Figure 4–4   Underhand Layup

erably the latter) as he begins his jump. If the ball is released with the shooting hand beneath the ball, the shot will be placed on the backboard softly and will stand a much greater chance of going in than shots taken with a power layup grip (knuckles facing the shooter). (See Figure 4–4.)

The Jump Shot

No offensive weapon plays a more important role in the game of basketball than the jump shot. The jump shot has done more to change basketball in recent years than any other single phase of the game. Jump shooters give defenses nightmares. In addition, the jump shot has provided one of the main reasons for the higher scores in basketball today. On the pro level, for example, even the best defenders cannot consistently hold opposing teams under 100 points per game. They simply cannot stop the versatile, ever-present jump shot.

In a typical game, more baskets are scored by jump shots than by all other shots together. The jump shot might be termed today's all-purpose shot because it can be taken from practically any angle by any player. For example, the *turnaround* jump shot is effective when the offensive player's back is to the basket. Jump shots can be taken while the player is standing still or on the move in practically any direction. (In *fallaway* jumpers the shooter is moving *away* from the basket.) The defender seldom knows in advance when the ballhandler is going to shoot, a fact that makes it virtually impossible to shut off his shot completely. The flexibility of the shot makes it difficult to defend against.

Usually, the jump shot is preceded by some form of movement, whether a dribble or foot or body motion. The first thing the jump shooter must do is position his feet in readiness for the jump. If the player is standing still, he may take a short step forward to create momentum for the jump. If he is dribbling laterally, he should pivot on the balls of his feet to square himself to the basket as he starts his jump. His knees must be bent, of course, and he should hold the ball with both hands close to his body. He should jump as high as possible, although the height of the jump is not as important as the timing involved and will vary with the shooter's distance from the basket.

As the shooter leaves the floor and rises into the air, he brings the ball up, keeping it close to his body until the ball is above his head at the top of his jump, or possibly even on the way down. (This position eliminates having too much body action in the shot.) Some jump shooters—Jerry Lucas was one—have been proficient in executing the jump shot from shoulder level, sighting over the top of the ball. However, the above-the-head position makes the shot more difficult for the defense to deflect if the shooter isn't 6′10″ like Lucas. In either position, the shooting elbow must be bent.

In executing the jump shot the player must remember (1) to make a proper stop before shooting and (2) to jump *up* rather than *forward*. Stopping before shooting will permit the jump shooter to go straight up in his jump and thus will afford him better body balance. Jumping forward in going up for the shot gives an alert defender the opportunity to draw a charging foul on the shooter. It may be better to lean backward slightly (and away from the defender) than to jump into the defender, although leaning backward slightly makes following one's shot to the boards more difficult.

The turnaround jump shot requires good footwork, since the shot is initiated with the shooter's back to the basket. The right-handed shooter uses his left foot as his pivot foot in executing a turnaround jump shot. He takes a crossover step in front of his body with his right foot, pivoting on the ball of his left foot. His body is now facing the basket. His right foot is then brought close to his left foot. (This motion can be accomplished in one step if the shooter's right foot can be placed close to his left foot without his losing balance.) A left-handed shooter uses his right foot as his pivot foot, stepping across his body to his right with his left foot in order to keep the ball protected by his body as he turns. (See Figures 4–5, 4–6, and 4–7.)

Figure 4–5   Jump Shot in Sequence (*a*)

Figure 4–6 Jump Shot in Sequence (*b*)

Figure 4–7 Jump Shot in Sequence (*c*)

The Hook Shot

Many big men have earned their reputation through effective use of the hook shot. (Kareem Abdul-Jabbar, for example, created the concept of the *sky hook*.) The step away from the defender and the actual release of the ball render the hook shot virtually impossible to stop. The ability to hook with either hand gives the offensive man that much greater an advantage.

In order to use hook shots effectively, a player must first develop his footwork and then his body positioning for the execution of the shot. When receiving the ball, the player should have both feet in contact with the floor. A short jump toward the ball will help make this possible. Jumping toward the ball allows either foot to be used as the pivot foot in initiating fakes with the head and shoulders and permits the receiver to go in either direction.

The right-handed hook shooter makes his first step with his left foot at an angle that maintains his distance from the basket. In other words, he steps away from his defender, but not from the basket. His left toe faces in the direction of this step to allow the right side of his body to move naturally. He should turn his eyes toward the basket as he takes the first step.

As his body swings around, the hook shooter raises his right knee high to allow a good follow-through. (He would raise his left knee if he were left handed.) The ball is held in both hands, with the left hand supporting the ball. As the ball is released to the right hand before shooting the hook shot, the left hand is raised to shoulder height and extended to protect the shot. The shooter's right hand moves under and behind the ball as his right arm begins a full arc upward. The movement of his body and arm will give a natural spin to the ball. (See Figure 4–8.)

The ball should be banked off the backboard when the shooter pivots to one side or the other from the middle of the lane, and it should be shot directly at the basket when the player is turning into the middle of the lane from the side. The distance the ball will have to travel in the air will determine the angle used on the backboard. When the shot is completed, the shooter's body should be in a follow-through position in much the same position as it would be if a set shot had been taken.

Set Shots and Free Throws

The two-hand set shot, once the favored shot in basketball, is largely a thing of the past. Pros Dolph Schayes and Clyde Lovellette were

Figure 4–8 Hook Shot

probably the last of the truly great two-hand set shooters. Contributing to this decline is the fact that many coaches have cut down
the distances from which they allow their players to shoot. In addition, the universality of the one-hand jump shot, with players able
to get a shot off much closer to the basket, and the players' increased
mobility and up-tempo play in recent years have all helped to foster
the demise of the two-hand set shot. The best that can be said for
two-hand set shots is that they increase a player's effective shooting
range.

In the two-hand set shot, the shooter's feet should be parallel
rather than staggered, and squared to the basket. The ball is held
in front of the body in both hands. The elbows are down at the
shooter's side rather than extended.

Both hands guide the ball toward the basket. In releasing the
ball, the player imparts backspin by an outward flipping motion of
his hands as they rotate toward a position in which the palms face

the basket. The arms should be extended fully toward a straight-arm position with the hands held high in a follow-through position.

Another of basketball's dinosaurs is the two-hand underhand free throw. With the exception of pro Rick Barry, one of the finest free-throw shooters in the history of basketball, nobody in recent years has made a mark shooting underhand free throws. This is an extremely accurate and extremely specialized form of shooting, and nowadays most players prefer to use a one-handed set shot when practicing free throws. The two-hand underhand free throw is a soft shot that often results in the ball rolling in even when shot slightly off line. In addition, muscle fatigue in this shot is not as detrimental as in other shots in which the ball must be supported from beneath before being released.

In preparing for this shot, the shooter places his feet in a position that is comfortable for him. His arms should be relaxed, and his elbows should be bent but resting at his sides. The fingers of both hands are pointed down as the ball is held in front below the hips. The hands should be slightly below the center of the ball with fingers spread. The shooter bends his knees as he lowers the ball, and the fingers of both hands move down and back toward his body.

As the upward shooting motion begins, the shooter's elbows should start forward before his hands. He guides the ball with his arms, and his hands follow the ball toward the basket as his wrists flip the ball.

The one-hand free throw is nothing more than a modfied one-hand set shot taken from the free-throw line. The shooter's feet can be parallel or staggered, depending upon which is most comfortable for the player. There should be relatively little knee action—just enough to gain a sense of rhythm. The shooting arm should be held chest high with the elbow bent, and there should be little arm action from this position. The less arm and leg action, the less chance there will be for mistakes to arise.

Follow-through should be full and complete. As the ball is released, the shooting hand, which initially was under the ball (wrist cocked) rather than behind it or on the side, should continue through until the wrists are extended fully and the palm of the shooting hand is facing the floor.

No other shot in basketball allows players the time or freedom of choice concerning style of delivery than a free throw. The distance is always the same, and there is no defender to worry about. Once the player has selected a style, he should *not* experiment with other styles. (This is truer for college players than high school or junior high school players.)

Even teams with poor field-goal percentages can be good free-throw shooting teams. Free throws often spell the difference between being in a game or out of it. When as many as 25 percent of the total points scored in games come as a result of free throws, they become a major factor in victories.

The most important factor in building a good free-throw shooting team is the team's ability to practice and concentrate on their free throws. Too often the players have little interest in them. It is the responsibility of both the coach and his players to understand the importance of free throws and to concentrate on them at practice. To use a rough parallel, free throws are to basketball what putting is to golf. Recall the old golfing adage, "You drive for show, but you putt for dough." Free-throw shooting is an important part of basketball, and concentration often determines the amount (or lack) of improvement a player can make.

5

Individual Defense

THE BASIC DEFENSIVE STANCE

One of the most popular descriptions of the defensive stance is found within the familiar litany "Feet spread, knees bent, tail down, back straight, and head and shoulders up." Some coaches teach their players to "keep your knees as wide apart as your shoulders," but we believe that doesn't go far enough. We believe that good defense, like a solidly constructed house, is built from the gound up. Therefore, we want our players to have their knees bent, of course, but we also want them to spread their *feet* as wide apart as they can get them. Their knees should be wider apart than their shoulders in order to create a low center of gravity and, as a result, to permit quick movement in any direction. (See Figure 5–1.) The easiest way to do this is to keep the feet spread. (Even in rebounding, which requires that the feet be relatively close together for gathering upward momentum and getting into the air quickly, the exaggerated spread of the feet serves a useful purpose before jumping—that of broadening the stance for blocking out and providing greater balance when physical contact occurs.)

Basketball is played from a bent-knee stance, with the bottom low. Up to a point, the lower the player's bottom—and the greater the degree of bend in the knees—the quicker the player's reaction to offensive movements. Sometimes a coach will tell his players to stand tall with arms outstretched to discourage passes inside when they are defending the post positions. However, players should be

Figure 5–1 Defensive Stance

discouraged from standing completely erect on defense. Anybody can stand up. If all that was required was somebody to stand up, a fifty-year-old fan from the stands would suffice.

One of the easiest ways for a player to simulate (that is, fake) a low defensive stance is to bend his back or lean forward at the waist, rather than bend his knees, spread his feet, and lower his bottom. (See Figure 5–2.) Leaning forward at the waist doesn't hurt

Figure 5–2 Incorrect Bending in the Defensive Stance

a player's legs as much as the low, sitting-down stance shown in Figure 5–1, but it doesn't afford much balance, quickness, or mobility, either. Leaning forward has absolutely nothing to do with improved anticipation or reaction. The perceptive coach will correct this posture whenever he sees it. If the player's torso is tilted forward, his eyes will naturally focus downward and he will be forced to compensate by craning his neck backward to see the action around him. All this can be avoided by making the players keep their backs straight in the first place.

The last part of the basic defensive stance, "head and shoulders up," follows naturally if the feet, knees, bottom, and back are given proper attention. Unless a player keeps his head up, he is not likely to follow the action as it evolves on the court.

Thus, we can see the basics of the defensive stance in its entirety: low, spread, and poised—in short, *coiled* like a giant spring. All of these elements are necessary if the defensive player is to anticipate and react swiftly to offensive movements. Make no mistake: assuming and maintaining an effective defensive stance is one of the most important fundamentals in basketball that a coach can teach his players.

Players who are not used to such physical exertion find the basic defensive stance difficult to achieve and even more difficult to maintain. Players not only must be taught the stance and movements associated with good defense but also must be drilled in these techniques constantly in order to extend their comfort zones. (A player's *comfort zone* is the level of performance he is most used to exhibiting; put another way, it is the highest level of physical exertion he can maintain without having fatigue impair his performance.) Extending the comfort zone is often associated with "getting in shape" and with running and conditioning drills designed to increase endurance. However, it also involves preparing players to achieve and maintain an effective defensive stance for long periods of time. Having the endurance to maintain a low, coiled defensive stance cannot be achieved through running drills. As a regular part of practice, coaches should provide a series of special drills in which players perform a variety of movement patterns in their defensive stances.

DEFENSIVE FOOTWORK

Once players are able to assume and maintain a stationary defensive stance, the coach's next step is to teach them to maintain the broad, low base while they move. This is accomplished by drilling the play-

Figure 5–3 Step-Slide Movement (*a*)

ers in the *step-slide* movement (Figures 5–3 and 5–4) and by constantly stressing the need for *sliding,* rather than running, in the
defensive coverage. Even when playing zone defense, players should
run only as a last resort. Running is not conducive to sudden changes
of direction, nor does it afford as good balance as sliding.

In sliding, the player should not allow his knees to come any
closer together than when he was in his stationary stance. Sliding
is done with the feet and lower leg (calves) rather than with the
thighs. We also stress keeping the feet in constant motion and keeping them near the floor. This movement is called *quick feet,* and we
believe it's the key to such aspects of defense play as drawing charging fouls, keeping pressure on the ballhandler, and maintaining
defensive pressure on men without the ball. A player cannot have
quick feet without a good defensive stance, and he cannot take large
steps if he keeps his knees wide apart.

Figure 5–4 Step-Slide Movement (*b*)

Before leaving the topic of footwork, we should mention that players should be drilled not only in sliding from a defensive stance but also in converting from a running stride to sliding and vice versa. Few, if any, skills in basketball do not depend on other skills for their execution. This certainly holds true for running, sliding, and other defensive footwork techniques. Smooth, quick conversions from sliding to running require practice, and the prudent coach who stresses both will also combine them in drills.

VARIATIONS OF DEFENSIVE STANCE

In guarding the dribbler, the defender may use either a *squared stance* (in which an imaginary line between his feet is perpendicular to the basket), a *boxer's,* or *staggered stance* (both of which require that one foot be placed ahead of the other). The squared stance is seen most often when the defender is either unsure of the dribbler's intentions or eventual direction, whereas the staggered stance is used to influence the dribbler in a particular direction.

Two situations may require a defender to stand tall rather than assume a wide, low stance. First, a defender may have to make himself as tall as possible in fronting a taller opponent at high or low post in order to deny passes inside. Second, when a dribbler has picked up the ball and terminated his dribble, the defender may have to close on the ballhandler and stand as tall as possible with hands held high to force lob passes that his teammates can pick off.

Using the Hands On Defense

Many coaches teach their players to keep their hands low when guarding the dribbler, with the palms upraised. This is probably as good a way as any, provided the defensive player is taught to keep his hands away from the dribbler (except when going for the ball) in order to avoid needless defensive fouls. In our defense, for example, we want the man on the ball to be practically inside the dribbler's jersey. We want him all over the dribbler, harassing him constantly, and we use six inches as a working maximum distance from his man. The defender can not stay that close to his man without fouling him if his elbows are by his sides and his hands are out toward the dribbler. Though we may advocate hands outstretched to the sides in an overguarded stance on the ball to stop the dribbler or discourage him from reversing to the middle or the other side of the court, we don't want the defender absentmindedly

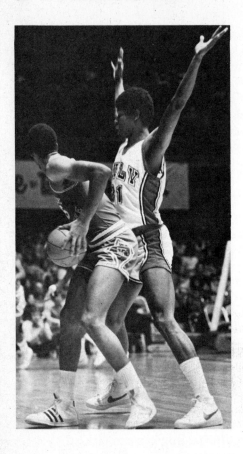

Figure 5–5   High-Hand Position on Defense

or needlessly handchecking the dribbler when he's not going after the ball or otherwise pursuing team goals. Generally speaking, handchecking is a sign of a lazy defense. Good defense is played first with the feet and only secondarily with the hands.

When the dribbler picks up the ball, his defender should keep one or both hands at the level of the ball. If the ballhandler holds the ball overhead, the defender should wave both hands overhead, perhaps leaping up and down in an effort to force a lob pass that can be intercepted. If the ball is held to one side, the defender should keep one hand at the level of the ball and one hand held high to prevent or deflect a pass over the head at the level of the ball. (See Figure 5–5).

When guarding a man at high or low post, players generally should extend their hands to full length to discourage passes, particularly when fronting. When guarding players one pass away from the ball, particularly in overplaying the passing lanes in pressure man-to-man or run-and-jump defense, players are often told by

Figure 5–6 "A Hand in the Passing Lane"

coaches to "keep a hand in the passing lane." This means that to discourage or deflect passes, the defender, while keeping his ball-side foot forward and overplaying toward the ball, must also thrust his ball-side hand into the passing lane (that is, into the invisible line between the ball and the player he's guarding). (See Figure 5–6.)

When guarding players two or more passes away from the ball, defenders should *point* their men and the ball—that is, point one hand at the ball and the other hand at the players they are guarding. This pointing technique forces defenders to divide their attention between the ball and their men and thus keeps them alert for changes in ball or court positions. In addition, it stresses the "sinking" aspect of such coverage, since a defender guarding his man too closely would have no need to point his man.

Overplaying the Dribbler

When overguarding, overplaying, or influencing the dribbler toward or away from a given area of the court, the defender must pay primary attention to the position of his own feet. In using sideline influence on the dribbler as shown in Figure 5–7, for example, the defender places his right, or *inside,* foot forward and drops his left, or *outside,* foot back in what is known as a staggered stance. The purposes behind this stance are (1) to facilitate quick movement to the defender's right if necessary to deny a reversal, and (2) to keep the stance open to cover the sideline movement and possible drive along the baseline.

The principle of overplaying is the same whether the defender is denying the dribbler access to a given area of the court or forcing

Figure 5–7   Sideline Influence (Overplaying)

Figure 5–8   Overplaying the Dribbler

him toward a certain area in order to reduce his options from that area: the foot on the vulnerable side is placed ahead of the other in a modified walking or running fashion (although the body is crouched in a low, spread, and balanced stance). (See Figure 5–8.)

Of course, the dribbler also can be overplayed toward the middle of the court, which is the case in most variations of man-to-man and zone defenses. In such cases, the defender's outside foot (that is, the one nearest the sideline or baseline) is placed ahead of the other foot to influence the dribbler away from the sideline or baseline.

Overplaying the Passing Lanes

When overplaying the passing lanes, a defender may be expected to either (1) "front" his man (facing him with hands upraised or spread-eagled) by playing between him and the ball, or, as is more often the case, (2) front his man partially by overplaying him to one side with an arm and a foot in the passing lane to discourage passes (See Figures 5–9 and 5–10.)

The distance the defender maintains from his man will vary with offensive movement, court position, the defensive player's skills, and coaching preferences, of course. However, it is generally

Figure 5–9 Fronting at the Wing

Figure 5–10   Partial Fronting at the Wing

considered unwise to guard the offensive player too closely outside. First, the pass is unlikely to be made, and therefore no steal or deflection will occur. Second, the offensive player is far more likely to use fakes to work himself open, particularly for backdoor passes.

In our pressure man-to-man defense, we teach our players to play "one step off the ball"—that is, one step behind the imaginary line (or toward the basket) between the ball and the men they're guarding and one-third of the distance between the ball from their men. In a two-guard offensive alignment, for example, this technique usually means playing one step off the line of the ball and two steps toward the ball. (See Figure 5–11.)

When a player away from the ball cuts behind his defender, as when a wing cuts through the lane to weak side, the defender should move into a close guarding position facing his man and fol-

Figure 5–11   Playing One-Step-Off-the-Ball Defense

lowing him with arms raised or outstretched to deflect possible passes. Because we prefer not to have to switch when we get back-doored, we insist that the defender whip his arm around and sprint to catch his man and cut him off if he gets the pass.

Covering the Posts

Our philosophy at UNLV concerning low-post coverage differs slightly from most other forms of man-to-man defense because of the unique nature of our needs. Take the case of a ballhandler passing from the point to a wing, as shown in Figures 5–12 and 5–13.

Before player number 34 passes to the wing, defender number 32 is fronting at low post for two reasons: to discourage the inside pass and, even more important, to deny the offense access to high post. Because we do not want our opponents to attack us from high post, we deny the pass by pressuring the ballhandler and fronting the low post. When the opponents are able to pass (or dribble) to

Figure 5–12   Low-Post Fronting

Figure 5–13   Low-Post Siding (V Fronting)

the wing, our low-post coverage changes to what we call *V fronting,* or *siding.* (See Figure 5–14.)

Traditional coverage entails overplaying from the inside out (i.e., forcing the pass toward the baseline if it is to be made) or fronting, which in this case means playing between the ball and the player at low post. In our man-to-man coverage, however, we po-

Figure 5–14   Siding (Closeup)

sition our defender between his man *and the sideline*. Essentially, we're fronting him from the sideline because, of all the offensive options available from the low-post position, the one we most want to deny with the ball at the wing is the low post player's cut to the ball-side corner. If the low-post player cuts to high post, we can continue to front him; if he clears to weak side to give the ballhandler at the wing room to drive, we can cover that too. If the low-post player cuts to the corner, however, our coverage will be reduced for one of three reasons: (1) the ballhandler may be able to force a double team from the baseline that will give the offensive team a resultant high-percentage open shot or baseline drive; (2) a pass-and-cut through the lane from the wing may permit the offensive team to attack us one-on-one from the baseline; or (3) if the ballhandler in the corner drives, his defender will never be able to reach the cutoff point in time to stop him; thus another defender will have to switch off to stop him. We feel that the easiest way to reduce the likelihood of this type of attack is to deny the offense access to the ball-side corner by siding.

Many coaches fail to have their players work on defensive footwork. Such practice is never wasted and is of paramount importance in teaching any style of individual defense. It is incorrect to assume that players will use proper footwork techniques naturally. Players must be taught and drilled to translate sliding movements into running (and vice versa) with the least possible loss of defensive control.

A good example of the importance of drill in reversing sliding and running movements may be seen in covering the ballhandler at the point in our pressure man-to-man defense. We want to play the ballhandler so closely that he'll have to turn and dribble toward one side or the other. When he begins dribbling, the defender should slide along with him from a close, overguarded position and be prepared to deny the reverse dribble to the middle or pass to weak side as he forces the ballhandler toward the sideline.

Sometimes, though, the ballhandler will elude his defender and drive toward the basket. When this happens, we expect the defender to stop sliding, pivot sharply, and sprint full speed to a point where he can cut off the dribbler.

The defender's first cutoff point is the ten-second mark along the sideline; that is, ideally the defender will drive his man to the sideline at or near the mark and force him to pick up the ball at that point. If he fails in this regard—which often happens, since the defender is conscious of denying the dribbler's reversal to the middle of the court, his second cutoff point is the corner. If he is unable to contain the dribbler at the ten-second mark, he will attempt to force

Figure 5–15   Steering the Dribbler Toward the Hash-Mark
Cutoff Point

Figure 5–16   Steering the
Dribbler Toward the Corner
Cutoff Point

Figure 5–17   The Low-Post
Cutoff Point

him toward the corner. If this effort fails, his final cutoff point is three feet outside the free-throw line along the baseline. When he reaches his cutoff point, he pivots and slides into position facing the dribbler. These movements—sliding, running, sliding—must be drilled into players if transition between them is to be quick, smooth, and efficient. (See Figures 5–15, 5–16, and 5–17.)

Covering Weak-Side Players

Techniques for covering weak-side players vary considerably among coaches; however, practically all systems in use today involve weak-side defenders sinking away from their men and toward the ball whenever their men are not primary receivers. In our system of man-to-man defense at UNLV, our weak-side defenders play at least one step off the ball. Of course, if their men cut behind them and across the lane, cut to a post position, or become primary pass receivers, the defenders will close as much as necessary to deny the pass.

Defenders more than one pass away from the ball do not need to assume the deep, wide-base stance of a defender on the ball; nevertheless, they should have their knees bent and open their stance to point their man and the ball.

Switching

Sometimes it is necessary for players to switch defensive responsibilities in order to retain or recover defensive control in a given situation. Defensive switching is usually associated with reacting to screens, but it is also used whenever an offensive player is either open with the ball or in a scoring position without the ball but is likely to receive a pass. In the latter case, awareness and anticipation on the court are the keys to defensive success in switching; after all, a defender is not likely to recognize a need to switch defensive responsibilities if he is unaware of the court positions of the other players.

We consider switching to be a last-ditch maneuver to be used only when other measures prove ineffective. To react to screens involving the ballhandler, for example, we prefer trapping the dribbler to the more passive act of switching. In addition, we do not employ switching in a situation concerning screens away from the ball. We always try to go over the top of screens, depending upon the pressure on the ballhandler to delay (or deny) the pass to the cutter while the defender catches him.

Nevertheless, many coaches teach switching techniques as re-
actions to screens, and though automatic switching is too passive
for our needs, we cannot (and would not) say that the technique is
inherently wrong. We don't spend much time working on zone defenses either, but that's not to say that zone defenses are unimpor-
tant. It's simply a matter of priorities, and in our particular system
of play we'd rather fight (through screens) than switch.

Switches may be either automatic or called; that is, players
may switch every time a screening situation arises, or they may
attempt to fight through screens and switch only when they cannot
go over the top of the screen. In both cases, it is important for the
player switching onto the ball to assume control quickly and deci-
sively. He cannot stand back and wait for the offensive player to
make a move or pass the ball. Similarly, the defender who has been
screened out must move quickly to a point between the screener and
the basket (or trap the dribbler with his switching teammate) or
face the possibility of a roll to the basket and subsequent layup by
the player setting the screen. (See Figures 5–18 and 5–19.)

Perhaps the most decisive way to effect the switch is for the
player picking up the cutter to step directly into his path as he
comes around the screen. Many times the switching defender can
draw a charging foul by stepping into the cutter's path as he sprints
around the screen. If the defender fails to draw the charging foul,
his position will still serve to stop the cutter's progress around the
screen, and the switching defender will then move into a close guard-

Figure 5–18   A Simple Defensive Switch (*a*)

Figure 5–19 A Simple
Defensive Switch (*b*)

ing position between his new man and the basket to deny the inside
pass. (If the cutter has *dribbled* around the screen, the switching
defender may move into a low stance in the dribbler's path and go
for the steal when the dribbler approaches him.)

Either player may call the switch if switching is not performed
automatically in response to screens. It is preferable, though, to
have the player who picks up the dribbler or cutter call the switch
rather than have the defender who receives the screen call out
"Switch!" when he sees that he cannot get through the screen. Because the defender being screened may not even see the screen until
it is too late to call it, having his teammate call out "Screen right!"
or "Screen left!" before calling the switch may help to avoid a defensive foul.

Going Over the Top of Screens

The term *going over the top of a screen* refers to the defensive technique of going around the screen on the same side of the player
setting the screen as the offensive player who receives the screen.
Switching is unnecessary when the defensive player is able to fight
through the screen. The most familiar alternative to switching
(other than going over the top of the screen) is *going behind the
screen*. However, this move is fraught with difficulty, since two players—the screener and the player guarding him—are between the
defender and the cutter, and the cutter thus has *two* men screening

Figure 5–20   Going Over the
Top of the Screen

for him whichever way he goes around the screen. (See Figures 5–20 and 5–21.)

The first step in going over the top of the screen involves knowing that a screen is being set or is going to be set. Players are sometimes coached to extend a hand behind them as they move, especially when guarding the dribbler, in situations in which screens are likely to occur. (It is unwise for players, while following cuts, to look away from their men in pursuit of passes for reasons that should be obvious.)

The second, and most important, aspect of going over the top of a screen is for the defender to take a quick step forward after the screen is set and just prior to the cutter's going around the screen. The rules provide that the player setting the screen must be sta-

Figure 5–21   Going Behind the
Screen

tionary when the cutter goes around the screen; thus, the defender's step forward into the cutter's path must occur *after* the screen is set and before the cutter is entirely past the screen. Because timing is all-important, the technique requires constant practice. In addition, the defensive player must also be willing to accept the contact involved. He is, after all, running the risk of being "sandwiched" between the two offensive players, thus it helps if he has an aggressive attitude about the screen. (That's why some coaches prefer to call this technique "fighting through" screens.)

We feel that combatting screens is largely a matter of attitude. Passive or unobservant players seldom deal forcefully with screens. Our philosophy of intensity and aggressive play at all times lends itself naturally to going over the top of screens, but we really have to motivate our players not to slack off and go behind the screen or switch. We look at this technique as a matter of pride. We ask the players, "Are you going to let your man go wherever he wants just because someone is in your way? If you let him do *that* to you, where will you draw the line at what you *won't* let him do to you?" We want our players to believe that, through constant hustle and alertness, they can control their men in *any* situation, including screens. Sometimes it may not be possible to get through the screen despite a player's best efforts, but we don't want to limit him beforehand by telling him to switch whenever he sees a screen. Even though it may be necessary in some situations, switching is always easier than going over the top of the screen. In our system, at least, we don't want our players looking for easy ways or short cuts. Other than a player's being 7 feet tall and extremely mobile, he has few short cuts to success. While the converse of the following statement may not hold true in every case, it is a fact that all teams that handle screens and picks well are likely to be outstanding defensively.

Blocking Out (Rebounding)

Height and vertical jumping ability are unquestionably important in basketball. A player whose standing vertical reach is eight feet, ten inches has a decided natural advantage over one whose reach is only seven feet, nine inches. The smaller player will have to jump some thirteen inches to match the standing reach of the taller player. When the taller man's vertical jump reaches skyward to thirty-six inches, as was the case with Wilt Chamberlain and Kareem Abdul-Jabbar, to name two famous tall leapers, the problem grows accordingly. How can opponents hope to rebound against such awesome performers?

Figure 5–22   Blocking Out

Figure 5–23   Going Up for the Rebound

Figure 5–24   Protecting the Ball

Figure 5–25   Tipping the Ball

They can begin by being willing to work as hard as necessary to get the rebound and by believing that every shot is going to be missed and preparing themselves accordingly. On defense, this technique necessitates maintaining one's natural inside position by blocking out, regardless of the amount of contact that occurs as the offensive player tries to go to the boards. Sometimes it may even involve sacrificing one's own chances of acquiring the rebound to keep the opponents' big man from getting inside. Offensive rebounding requires a sense of anticipation, a knowledge of where the shot was taken from (and thus where it is likely to rebound), and the abilities to get to the basket and to time one's leap to coincide with the ball's coming off the rim or board.

Statistical surveys have shown that over 70 percent of all missed shots rebound long—that is they carom off the other side of the board at an angle equal to that of their approach. Knowing this and knowing that perimeter shots stay in the air for two to three seconds, depending upon the shot's arc, the offensive rebounder can time his break to the proper area around the basket without watching the ball in its flight to the basket.

When a rebounder reaches a desirable area near the basket, his first objective is to "secure the area," or claim it as his own by widening his stance, spreading his elbows to maximum extension, and resisting contact by opponents attempting to force their way into his area. In essence, blocking out is a way of equalizing rebounding disadvantages as well as improving one's own superiority under the boards. Wes Unseld, one of basketball's finest offensive rebounders, although only 6'7", cites the keys to successful rebounding as "getting there first" and then maintaining an inside position through spreading your body over as wide a base as possible and fighting the contact as it arises.* Unseld considers offensive rebounding not necessarily easy, but at least feasible, since familiarity with the shooting habits of teammates can help an aggressive rebounder position himself to grab off errant shots, or tip-in shots as they come off the rim. (See Figures 5–22, 5–23, 5–24, and 5–25.)

* Earl Monroe and Wes Unseld, *The Basketball Skill Book* (New York: Atheneum Press, 1973), pp. 87–93.

II

Individual to Three-Man Drills

6

Conditioning Drills

Conditioning is a vital part of every team's preparation. A team may lose games because it is not blessed with good rebounders, ballhandlers, or shooters, but there is simply no excuse for losing games because the players aren't in shape. Conditioning is one aspect of a team's performance over which the coach has complete control. No matter how inexperienced or unskilled the players are or their style of play, they should be in condition to play with the same freshness and intensity in the latter stages of games as they did in the first quarter. To this end, conditioning may be seen as an overloading process, preparing players as if they were to play five or six quarters rather than four or three halves instead of two.

The question sometimes arises as to how much running a team should do. Although there can be no definite answer to this question, it is safe to say that *a team cannot do too much running*; too little running in practice will leave a team vulnerable to fatigue in the latter stages of games.

Conditioning may be divided into two categories, running to build endurance and running to build speed and strength (power). While interrelated, the two are not exactly the same: although power running builds endurance, strictly endurance running (e.g., jogging) does not necessarily increase speed or quickness to any great extent.

ENDURANCE RUNNING

The conditioning provided by distance running is as much mental as physical. When players have been conditioned psychologically to accept a daily mile or so of running at practice, they find it easier to accept other hardships that are necessary to building a winning basketball program. Once the players discover that running a mile or so, while tiring and painful to a certain extent in the earliest stages of training, will not prove fatal or permanently damaging to their legs or lungs, they should find it relatively easy to accept other running drills, especially when the drills are specifically related to their basketball-skills development.

POWER RUNNING

Power running may be defined as *full-speed running for short distances*. These distances usually constitute the length of the court or farther, as in wind sprints, but the "full-speed" aspect may consist of a series of starts and stops that cover only a few feet at a time. For example, the coach may use regular wind sprints but include a series of whistle blasts to start and stop players on command. The sudden starts and stops involved will build leg strength as effectively as any other form of running. Basketball is a game of sudden starts and stops, of transitions and unexpected turnovers, and power-running drills cannot but help a team in its preparation for games.

Speed plus strength equals power. Drills or scrimmaging featuring power running should be included in every practice session. In addition to improving strength, speed, and endurance, skills-related power running increases players' high-speed ballhandling proficiency, an important aspect of preparation even for teams that use a deliberate style of play. (Note: defensive drills and full-court scrimmaging can also provide excellent power conditioning.)

In order to play most effectively on offense and defense, players should be coached to extend the limits of their comfort zone; that is, they should be conditioned mentally and physically to accept the presence of pain and fatigue in practice in order to play aggressively in games without being overcome by fatigue. Power running builds strong legs not only for fast breaking and getting back quickly on defense but also for rebounding (including positioning and blocking out), defense, and other phases of the game. Power running benefits players in all phases of the game of basketball.

ENDURANCE DRILLS

Laps

Distance running in the form of laps around the gym floor is perhaps the most primitive of conditioning drills in basketball. In the form of jogging, running laps may or may not increase leg strength, but they will improve cardiorespiratory efficiency. Unfortunately, coaches who want their players to run at a pace somewhat faster than jogging may have difficulty describing the desired pace to their players. To simply say "Run faster!" is somewhat ambiguous, especially to young players unused to running at all. Describing the pace as "faster than a trot and slower than full speed" is equally confusing. Moreover, human nature dictates that most players will opt for the minimum rate.

     Dribbling while running laps can serve a two-fold purpose: help to break the monotony of seemingly endless laps around familiar scenery and also provide players with additional practice in a phase of the game in which they sorely need practice.

Roadwork

Some coaches take their players outside for running, either on the school's track or on the open road. The second option is risky for obvious reasons: on the road, the players are largely unsupervised and thus may be victimized by traffic, pranksters, dogs, or sudden urges to stop at a local convenience store. Insurance companies and local boards of education would probably take a dim view of this kind of activity.

     We've found that running around a track increases output drastically over running around a gym. Being "lapped" in the gym is not nearly as embarrassing as it is when running around a track or football field. (One lap around a high school gym floor measures 93 yards, while the perimeter of a high school football field measures slightly more than 350 yards.)

     A coaching acquaintance took his team outside to run one day while the gym floor was being repaired. The players ran a mile around the football field—slightly more than five laps—and when finished, they were all breathless and had sore and tight leg muscles, although they'd been running the same distance in the gym every day for more than two months. In the gym, the same amount of running had long since ceased to tax them. Our friend concluded that their pace increased drastically outside because their familiar visual cues were gone and because being "lapped" outside was a greater stigma than it was in the gym.

Paced Laps

If your team is going to run laps, one way to speed up their completion is to designate one player to be last, with everyone else expected to stay ahead of him or at least to avoid being lapped by him. The player selected as the pacesetter should not be the fastest man on your team (no one will be able to keep up with him) or the slowest, since everyone else will lap him.

The converse of this tactic, putting the slowest players at the front and expecting them to stay ahead of the others, will not work. Instead of speeding up the slower players, this strategy will show down the faster ones.

Progressive Laps

Progressive laps are superior to regular laps in building or increasing endurance. Progressive laps feature changed speeds, always desirable in conditioning drills, and build speed and strength as well as stamina.

To run progressive laps, all the players should line up and run in single file. They may run at any pace they wish for the entire distance except that, whenever a player becomes the last one in line, he must sprint full speed to the front of the line. Then he slows down to his former pace again.

Regular, paced, and progressive laps are time consuming and may detract from practice in situations where time is valuable; however, they may be a necessary evil.

Interval Sprint Laps

Interval sprint laps are performed more easily outdoors than in the gym, but they can be used effectively anywhere. The players alternate between jogging and sprinting, with the intervals measured either by distance or time. In the gym, for example, players can sprint along the sidelines and jog along the baselines or jog for thirty seconds and sprint for thirty seconds. Either way, the benefits of running interval sprint laps are likely to be greater than those gained from running regular laps.

We do not use laps or distance running per se to get our players in shape. Instead, we rely on our rigorous competitive drills and controlled scrimmaging to build power and endurance. Running laps does nothing but improve endurance. Intensive drills and controlled scrimmaging improve defensive and offensive skills as they get the players in shape.

POWER RUNNING DRILLS

Wind Sprints

Wind sprints consist simply of running the length of the court at top speed, resting momentarily, then sprinting full speed back to the other end of the court. Anyone who thinks that this kind of running is easy hasn't tried it. Some coaches use this drill in early preseason practice to find out who's dedicated to basketball and who's coming out for the team because they think they'd look good in a uniform. Other coaches use wind sprints as punishment for players who cut practices or classes. However, most coaches use wind sprints because they *will* get players in shape to play basketball.

Start-and-Stop Sprints

If wind sprints are tough, start-and-stop sprints are worse. The players line up along the baseline and run forward at the coach's whistle. On the next whistle, they stop immediately, usually in a low, balanced (that is, defensive) stance, ready to sprint again on the next whistle. Thus, they start and stop and start and stop their way downcourt on every whistle, resting only when they reach the opposite baseline.

Ladder, or Suicide, Drill

Some coaches believe that the ladder drill is the most fiendishly effective power-running exercise devised for basketball, with the possible exception of running up and down bleachers. Players line up along the baseline and on a given signal, begin sprinting downcourt. Upon reaching the opposite baseline, they touch the floor with one or both hands and then turn and sprint back to the starting line. Without pausing (except to touch the floor beyond the starting line), they turn, sprint back to the opposite extended free-throw line,

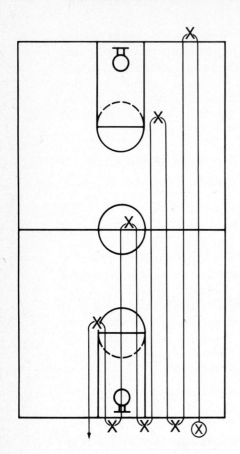

Figure 6–1   Ladder, or Suicide, Drill

touch, sprint to the baseline, touch, sprint to the half-court line, touch, sprint to the baseline, touch, sprint to the nearer free-throw line, touch, and sprint across the baseline. (See Figure 6–1.)*

We've just described one ladder, or suicide, drill. Multiply it by five, or eight, or ten in the course of one practice session, and you have some of the most exquisite agonies in basketball short of a sprained ankle. Run the drill on a daily basis, and you have some of the most exquisitely conditioned athletes in basketball.

The only way to make suicides more difficult than they already are is to add a time limit of, say, twenty-five to thirty seconds in which everyone has to finish. But don't expect the players to do this drill more than once or twice per session within that time limit.

---

* Players always run along the same route up and down the court, not the route shown in Figure 6–1. This drill is very hard to diagram.

Instead of having players touch the floor, some coaches prefer to use the suicide drill to work on high-speed dribbling. Obviously, times are much slower when the players are dribbling, thus "dribbling suicides" are not timed.

We run our suicide drills slightly differently—that is, *across* the court. We line up the players along the sideline and on the coach's signal, they begin running back and forth across the court, touching beyond the sideline every time. They run for one minute at a time, and every player on the team is expected to make at least seventeen touches. This means crossing the court and touching every three and one-half seconds for one minute. If any of the players fail to reach seventeen touches all have to line up and do this drill again immediately. For the final touch, we'll have the players dive across the finish line so as to prepare them to go on the floor after loose balls in games. (We like to say that, whether we can control the boards or not, *the floor is ours!*)

Sometimes we'll do this drill two to three times in a single practice session. In combination with the rigorous and demanding one-on-one, two-on-two, and three-on-three competitive drills we use, the ladder drill prepares our players superbly for the intense, high-speed game we play. Our players are highly disciplined, and we like to think that a positive attitude toward conditioning falls under the category of self-discipline. Our players have often remarked that games are easy, compared to our grueling practices. We feel this attitude should be every coach's goal.

Three-Man Weave

The three-man weave, or figure-eight passing drill, has always been popular with coaches. It is sometimes used as a conditioning drill, although its main purpose is to drill players in high-speed ballhandling. In addition to conditioning and practicing high-speed ballhandling, however, the three-man weave is also excellent for teaching young or unskilled players to concentrate on moving in predetermined routes while watching teammates and passing the ball. It can also help to teach players to change speeds while running, through cuts behind the pass receiver, and speeding downcourt after passing.

The players line up in three lines out of bounds behind the baseline. The wing players—O2 and O3 in Figure 6–2—may set up as close as the edges of the free-throw lane or as wide as the corners, depending upon their skills and coaching preferences. On O1's signal, O2 and O3 begin moving straight downcourt, anticipating O1's

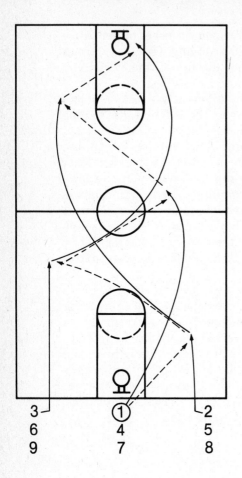

Figure 6–2 Three-Man Weave, or Figure Eight

pass. (It is important to teach young players to continue downcourt in a straight line until they receive a pass, or else they'll all run together in the middle.) O1 passes to O2, cuts behind him, and continues downcourt in a straight line. O2 passes crosscourt to O3, cuts behind him, and continues downcourt in a straight line. O3 passes crosscourt to O1, cuts behind him, and continues downcourt in a straight line. This sequence—pass, cut behind, move downcourt in a straight line until receiving another pass—continues until one of the three players is close enough to the basket to shoot the layup. Players should speed up every time they cut crosscourt and behind a teammate in the three-man weave, since the player who will pass to them will be farther downcourt than they are when the previous pass is made.

It takes some time for unskilled players to memorize the sequence of cuts, passes, and receptions. Keys that will facilitate progress include: (1) the same player who passed to you the first time will pass to you every time; (2) you will pass to the same player every time; and (3) you don't cut across the middle of the court until after you've passed the ball. The most common mistake in the three-man weave is cutting to the middle to receive the pass.

Three-Man Weave With Dribble. The regular three-man weave is a pass-and-cut drill. Adding a single dribble to each player's responsibility makes the drill into a dribble, pass-and-cut pattern. The players set up in three lines, but the wings set up wider than before (Figure 6–3). O1 dribbles once, passes to O2, cuts behind him, and

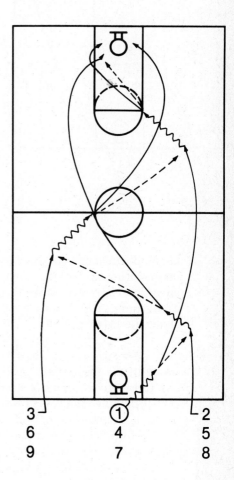

Figure 6–3   Three-Man Weave
With Dribble

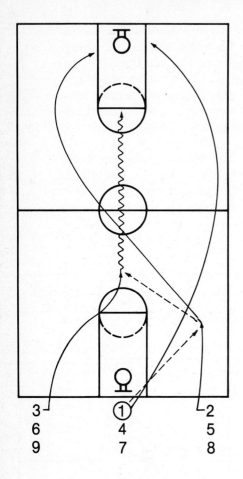

Figure 6–4   Three-Man Weave
as a Fast-Break Drill

heads downcourt. O2 dribbles once, passes crosscourt to O3, cuts
behind him, and heads downcourt. O3 catches O2's pass, dribbles
once, passes crosscourt to O1, cuts behind him, and heads downcourt.
The sequence is repeated until one of the players is in position to
shoot the layup.

Three-Man Weave as a Fast-Break Drill. When used as a training drill for fast breaking, the three-man weave usually includes
two passes to establish the ball at the middle of the court. Then the
player dribbles the rest of the way downcourt. Wings O2 and O3 set
up wide, as shown in Figure 6–4. O1 passes to O2, swings wide
behind him, and continues downcourt at full speed. O2 passes to O3,
cuts behind him, and continues downcourt. O3 slides toward the
middle to receive O2's pass and then dribbles downcourt as O1 and

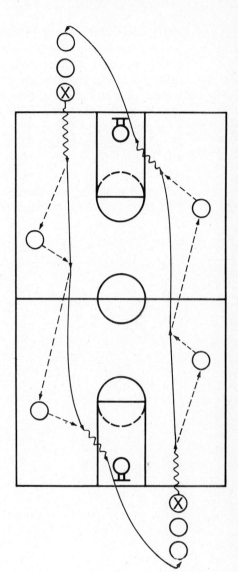

Figure 6–5 Full-Court Sideline Passing Drill

O2 fill the passing lanes. Obviously, O1 and O2 must run full-speed to catch up with O3 and fill the passing lanes along the sideline.

Full-Court Sideline Passing Drill

Instead of passing and cutting as in the three-man weave, the full-court sideline passing drill features one player following a fixed route downcourt along the sideline until he is able to shoot the layup. The ballhandlers at both ends dribble once or twice, then pass to a player stationed out of bounds at the ten-second mark, and continue along the sideline for a return pass. They then pass to a second player stationed downcourt. Upon receiving the second return pass, the players dribble to the basket for a layup, retrieve the ball, and pass to the first person in line at that end of the court. Then they move to the back of the line at that end of the court. Junior high teams with small or young players may have to station three players along the sidelines instead of two. In any case, the players should be encouraged to run at top speed as they pass the ball and receive return passes. (See Figure 6–5.)

7

Passing Drills

Offensive players may be either stationary or moving when they pass the ball. Beginning players prefer stationary passes, of course, but game situations often rule out stationary passes. Young players should be taught that the fundamental skills involved in passing remain the same, regardless of whether they are moving or standing still. The chest pass, two-hand overhead pass, baseball pass, bounce pass and, underhand (shovel) pass are the basic passes in basketball. Of these only the chest pass, two-hand overhead pass, and perhaps the bounce pass should be used by unskilled players. Coaches should discourage all but their most outstanding ballhandlers from using baseball passes or shovel passes. Shoulder passes (bringing the ball up near the shoulder with both hands before passing) should be strongly discouraged, since they deny the passer access to passing lanes on the other side of his body.

STATIONARY PASSING DRILLS

The coach should use stationary passing drills to emphasize selected basic passing skills prior to teaching these skills through passing drills featuring movement.

Semicircle Passing Drill (Two Balls)

This drill teaches players not to look where they're passing the ball, but to use their peripheral vision to locate teammates.

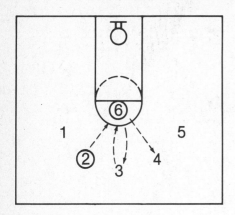

Figure 7–1   Semicircle Passing Drill

One player—O6 in Figure 7–1—faces four to six players arranged in a semicircle (or straight line) facing him. He holds a basketball. One of the players facing him holds a second ball. On a given signal, O6 passes to O3, and O2 passes to O6. O3 passes back to O6, who by now has passed to O4. O4 passes to O6, who has passed to O5 and so forth. Thus, the two balls are constantly in motion, with O6 passing to each outside man in turn and the outside players returning O6's passes as they receive them.

If O6 watches the pass receiver rather than the player who is passing the other ball back to him, he is likely to be hit in the head by the pass. Thus, he learns quickly and convincingly to watch the man passing to him rather than his intended receiver. (In games, he would be watching the defensive player.)

Circle Passing Drill. A player who can perform the semicircle passing drill can as easily do the circle passing drill as long as he remembers to pivot or turn continually in the direction of passes.

The drill is exactly like the semicircle passing drill, except that all the players on the team position themselves in a circle surrounding the player in the middle.

Four-Ball Circle Passing Drill. In the four-ball version of the circle passing drill, *two* players stand back-to-back in the middle of the circle, each controlling two balls as before. The two players must rotate in the same direction, of course, to avoid colliding.

This drill is much easier than it looks, and the only mistakes likely to occur are those resulting from dropped passes. Receivers must return passes promptly.

Keepaway

This drill invokes memories of childhood games. Put one player in the middle of a circle with instructions to get the ball or touch the player who has it, and you have an activity that will lighten the gloomiest practice session, especially one made up of junior high school players. Vary the passes. For example, require all passes to be bounce or overhead passes, and you have a self-motivating activity with concentrated practice on a specific skill. And best of all, it's fun!

The variations are endless: two "it" players in the middle or two balls being passed around the outside or changing the "it" players with every dropped pass. The only rule is that no player may pass to the man on his immediate right or left.

Faking

One of the most important, yet often overlooked, aspects of a team's passing game is faking. For example, in Figure 7–2, the ballhandler has dribbled to the top of the circle to freeze the outside defenders in position. His teammates are open at the wing positions, provided he can get the ball to either of them. If he throws a lob pass, however, an inside defender will be able to cover the pass receiver; and if the point guard throws a bounce pass, an outside defender will likely deflect or steal it. (Until he passes the ball, the inside defenders are frozen in position also, since they do not know to which side he intends to pass until he commits himself.)

Figure 7–2 Forcing the Outside Double Team

Lob passes aside, then, how can the point guard get the ball to a wing player before the inside defender gets outside to cover it? The point guard can do this by faking a bounce pass and by bringing the ball up suddenly and whipping a pass by the defender's ear, as this man drops his arms.

To practice stationary faking, position two players facing each other on either side of the free-throw lane, with a defender two or three feet away from, and slightly to one side of, the player with the ball. The object of the drill is like that of keepaway: to pass beyond the defensive player to the player on the other side of the lane. Care must be taken, however, to communicate to the players that they are *not* playing keepaway and that rapid passing back and forth by the outside players is undesirable. The defensive player should be given time to position himself to defense the pass.

MOVING PASSING DRILLS

Perhaps we should point out at this point that every passing drill is also a pass receiving drill. Young players should be taught not to point their fingers toward the ball when catching passes, especially when the ball has been thrown hard, in order to avoid painfully jammed fingers.

Two-Line Passing Drill

This drill teaches players to throw the ball softly when they are close to the pass receiver. Two groups of players face each other in single file. One ball is used. The player in front with the ball passes

Figure 7–3   Two-Line Passing Drill

Figure 7–4   Two-Circle Passing Drill

to the first player in the other line and continues to the back of that line. All players then move forward slowly, catching the pass, passing to the next man in the opposite line, and moving to the back of that line. (See Figure 7–3.)

Two-Circle Passing Drill. This drill is a variation of the two-line passing drill. (See Figure 7–4.) Again, one ball is used. The players are grouped in two circles, the size of which depends upon the number of players in the groups. On signal, both groups begin trotting either clockwise or counterclockwise and passing the ball from circle to circle, with both groups moving in the same direction.

Downcourt Passing Drill

Two players stand at the baseline on either side of the free-throw line, with one of them holding the ball. On command, they begin running downcourt, passing the ball between them. When they reach the other end, the one in shooting position shoots the layup. It's a simple drill that can be used to teach players to move the ball quickly, catch passes and return them without committing traveling violations.

Variation: Three players stand along the baseline, say, twelve to fifteen feet apart. On signal, they run full-speed downcourt, passing the ball between themselves, but staying in their lanes rather than cutting as in the three-weave. Though the objective of the drill is identical to that of the two-player drill, the three-player variation

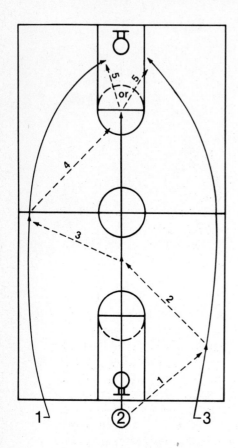

Figure 7–5 Downcourt Passing Drill (Three-Man Variation)

provides players with better practice at following their lanes down-court at high speed while watching the ballhandler.

O2 passes to O3, who immediately passes back to O2. O2 passes to O1, who does the same. The pattern continues—pass to a wing, pass to the middle, and pass to the other wing—until a cutter is in position to shoot the layup. (The player in the middle stops at the free-throw line.) (See Figure 7–5.)

Instead of passing first to one side, then the other, the player in the middle may be instructed to pass to whichever side he wishes, especially if the players occupying the lanes along the sideline tend to take their eyes off the ballhandler in order to watch where they're going.

Four-Corner Passing Drill

All the players except O1, the player with the ball, line up in the four corners of the half court. O1 positions himself midway between

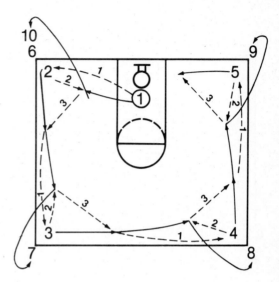

Figure 7–6 Four-Corner
Passing Drill

O5 and O2. O1 passes to O2, who remains in his corner until he
returns the ball to O1. O2 then cuts toward the line to his right,
receives a second pass from O1, and passes to O3 in the next line.
O1 goes to the back of O2's original line.

O3 stands still until he makes a return pass to O2, then cuts
toward O4's corner to receive a second pass from O2. O2 moves to
the rear of O3's original line. The sequence may continue for as long
as desired. (See Figure 7–6.)

Variation: One way of varying the drill to make it faster is
to add one or more balls and thus to have two, three, or four basketballs going at the same time. The drill is colorful and exciting

Figure 7–7 Four-Corner Passing Drill (Four Balls)

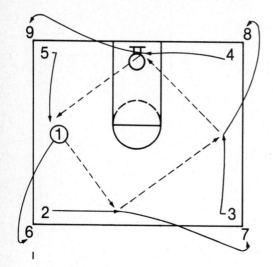

Figure 7–8 Four-Corner
Passing, Drill (Variation)

in this form as long as the players don't drop a pass or forget their
sequence of movements. When one player makes a mistake, everyone has to stop and wait for him to start over at that point.

All that is needed to set up two or more players to pass and
cut at the same time is to move them to positions midway between
any two adjacent corners and give them a ball. In the four-ball
version, then, players would occupy all four of the positions shown
in Figure 7–7.

Variation: These drills may be varied further by reversing
the direction of the passes. For instance, instead of returning passes,
players catch the ball and pass to the next line while cutting. (See
Figure 7–8.)

O1 has the ball. O2 cuts toward O3's line. O1 passes to O2 and
goes to the back of his line. O3 cuts toward O4's line. O2 passes to
O3 and moves to the rear of his line. The pattern may be reversed.

The only problem with this drill is that sometimes younger
players cannot throw the ball hard enough or far enough to reach
the cutters. In such cases, the lines may be brought closer together
to facilitate the longer passes.

Four-Corner Pivot-and-Pass Drill

The four-corner pivot-and-pass drill, although simple in execution,
is a precision drill emphasizing dribbling, reverse pivoting, passing,
and timing.

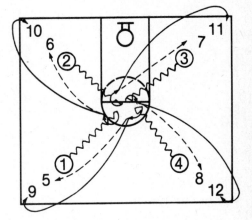

Figure 7–9　Four-Corner Pivot-
and-Pass Drill

The drill looks best when all four players start at the same
time, dribble in cadence, and stop and point their basketballs toward
the middle before reverse pivoting and passing. When the players
stop at the middle, their forward foot should be the foot on the side
to which they intent to turn. (See Figure 7–9.) For example, in
reverse pivoting to his left the ballhandler picks up his dribble and
stops with his left foot forward, steps backward and to his left toward
the passing line on his left with his right foot, passes to the next
player in line, and moves to the back of that line.

This drill may be used strictly as a dribbling drill by substi-
tuting dribbling for passing. In a sequence of movements similar to
that shown in Figure 7–9, the ballhandlers dribble toward the middle with their right hands, stop with their left feet forward, reverse
pivot, and continue their dribble with their left hands to the next
line. (See Figures 7–10 and 7–11.)

Figure 7–10　Footwork, Pivot-and-Pass Drill (*a*)

Figure 7–11 Footwork, Pivot-and-Pass Drill (*b*)

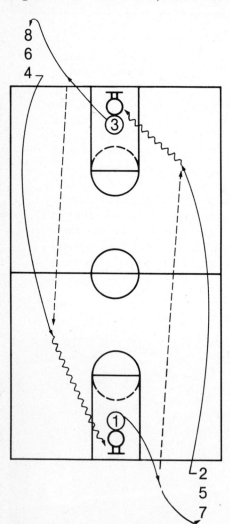

Figure 7–12 Baseball Pass Layup Drill

Baseball Pass Layup Drill (Full Court)

Although many coaches frown on their players' throwing baseball passes because of the large incidence of turnovers associated with their use, the drill shown in Figure 7–12 is an excellent conditioner as well as a drill providing practice in inbounding the ball quickly after scores.

O1 and O3 begin the drill by standing under the basket. On signal, they rush out of bounds and throw a one-handed, overhand baseball pass to O2 and O4 who are breaking downcourt. After catching the passes, O2 and O4 dribble to the basket and shoot layups. O5 and O6 rebound the shots and step out of bounds as O7 and O8 break downcourt.

8

Dribbling Drills

Ballhandling skills, like shooting skills, are not generally developed in the gymnasium during practice. The coach may sharpen his players' skills to a certain extent with dribbling and passing drills, but the real responsibility for improved ballhandling rests with the individual players: if they aren't dedicated to practicing on their own, at home or on the playground, their improvement in individual skills will be slow and negligible at best.

In addition, the time available for practicing individual skills is usually limited, since team skills and strategies must also be learned and rehearsed. Most coaches feel that they cannot afford to devote the major portion of every practice session to individual skills-development throughout even the preseason phase of practice. (The one exception is in coaching unskilled junior high or high school players.)

Ballhandlers should be taught to use two types of dribbling, protective dribbling and high-speed dribbling. They also should be taught change-of-pace dribbling that involves protective and high-speed dribbling in all directions. Protective dribbling is used whenever a defensive player is near the ballhandler and is controlling his progress. When protecting his dribble, the ballhandler turns his body (and the ball) away from the defensive player. As he dribbles, he slides in *step-together, step-together* fashion, with the ball near his back foot (the foot farthest away from the defender.)

127

High-speed dribbling, on the other hand, is aggressive. The dribbler, moving at nearly top speed in the absense of tight defensive coverage or overplaying, has no need to protect the ball by keeping it back and away from the defender. Instead, he keeps the ball in front of him and outside his body, pushing the ball ahead of him as he dribbles.

DRILLS

Rocker Dribble

One of the first skills inexperienced players should master is how to move the ball around in dribbling without pushing it straight down toward the floor. The rocker dribble will help them learn this important skill.

The ballhandler stands with legs together, holding the ball in front of, and to the right of, his body (in right-handed dribbling). He swings the ball down so that it strikes the floor beside him. Since the ball will rebound behind him, the dribbler reaches back to catch it and allows it to rise naturally in his hand. He then pushes the ball back toward the same spot where it landed originally and reaches out again to catch it in front of him.

This *rocking motion* can also be performed by dribbling the ball from side to side. The easiest way to explain this is to tell players to dribble the ball from side to side in front of them, using both hands in turn. Then tell them to do the same thing with their right hand only. Players should also do these rocker drills while walking, skipping or trotting.

Triangle Dribble

The object of this drill is simple: to dribble the ball around the body in three dribbles. It's easy, provided the dribbler has mastered the rocker dribbling movement, and extremely difficult if he has to push the ball straight down to control his dribble. The dribbler holds the ball in his right hand diagonally in front of him and swings it down and back, catches it low off the dribble in his right hand behind his back, and pushes it to his left side. He then catches it in his left hand by raising his hand slightly to gain control of the ball and bounces the ball toward his right side in front of his body.

The direction and order of dribbles can be reversed, of course. The only real problem arises when the dribbler tries to start the drill by dribbling straight backward instead of diagonally; if he does this, he'll have to palm the ball on his second right-handed dribble to get it around his body. Even then he may have trouble controlling the third (left-handed) dribble.

Variation: Much easier to perform than the previous drill are triangle dribbles around either leg (with the legs spread, of course). This drill is excellent for practicing low fingertip-control dribbling. Like the previous drill, the change of direction involved here provides the player with practice in dribbling with his weak hand.

Figure-Eight Dribble

This drill is exactly like the variation of the triangle dribble, except that the dribbler weaves his way in and out of his legs in figure eights instead of going the same way around each leg.

Variations: Though most coaches use the figure-eight dribble to practice low fingertip-control dribbling, it has other applications as well. The dribbler, standing erect, can start out by making three dribbles around each leg as in the triangle dribble previously described (only here dribbling in figure eights) and progress to using only *two* dribbles to get around each leg. (Dribble diagonally back on the first dribble, through the legs on the second dribble, back on first, through on second, and so forth.) When the dribbler has conquered the two-dribble sequence, he can try *one-dribble* figure eights. These require that the dribbler palm the ball on each dribble and also exercise a great deal of *ball control*, the main goal of all dribbling drills.

Pretzel Dribble

We can thank Pete Maravich for the pretzel dribble, one of the many innovative ballhandling drills he has invented. In the pretzel dribble, the ballhandler first spreads his legs in order to dribble between them and then dribbles four times, using his right and left hands alternately. The sequence of the four dribbles is as follows: right hand in front of the body, left hand in front of the body, right hand behind the leg, and left hand behind the leg—these are all done by the player dribbling straight down with the ball between his legs.

Walking Pretzel Dribble

In the walking pretzel dribble, the player dribbles between his legs on every step. (For increased speed, the player can skip rather than walk.)

There are two ways to perform the walking pretzel dribble: (1) with his left foot forward and the ball in his right hand, the player dribbles the ball in front of his right leg, catches it with his left hand as he steps forward with his right foot, and then dribbles the ball in front of his left leg, and so forth; or (2) with his right foot forward and the ball in his right hand, the player dribbles the ball behind his right leg, catches it with his left hand as he steps forward with his left foot, and then with his left hand dribbles the ball behind his left leg, and so forth.

Wave Dribble

The wave dribble is borrowed from football, where it is used to sharpen players' agility and reaction time. In basketball, it is an excellent preseason drill, an indispensable means of offering concentrated practice in dribbling with one's weak hand.

Players set up in four or five lines out of bounds, with the first player in each line holding a basketball. The coach or a manager stands at the half-court line. On signal, the players dribble forward until the coach signals a change of direction to the left, right, or backward. Whenever a player stops watching his hand, the coach signals a change of direction. Some coaches use broad arm and hand movements to signify changes of direction. Others prefer small finger signals to force players to watch them closely rather than the ball or their teammates. (Players should *slide* rather than run in this drill or speed-dribble forward and slide in the other directions.)

Tag

One player is designated "it." He must maintain control of his dribble before and after tagging another player. The other players, who all are dribbling basketballs, try to stay away from "it" within a half-court area. Players may not leave the half-court area to avoid being tagged. If they lose control of the ball while being chased, they become "it" even if they are not tagged. Tagging back is optional. The no-tagging-back version increases movement by all the players.

The "it" player may be allowed to dribble with either hand, while everyone else dribbles with their weaker hand, since without this help some players would never catch their teammates. Players may also be required to alternate dribbling between their right and left hands.

Capture the Flags

For this drill, every player must have a basketball and a *flag* (a rag, towel, or piece of cloth) tucked into his shorts in back. At least six inches of flag should be showing in back.

Players are confined to one half of the court. On signal, they begin moving about and dribbling, while also attempting to capture other players' flags as they protect their own flags. As players have their flags captured, they retire from the game. The winner is the last player remaining with his flag still tucked into his shorts.

As the number of players left in the game dwindles, the boundaries of their dribbling area should be reduced. As in the other drills, dribbling only with one's weak hand or alternating between right- and left-handed dribbling may be required.

One-Dribble Layup From the Top of the Circle

This drill stresses the importance of pushing the ball ahead when dribbling at high speed rather than pounding the ball incessantly at one's side. From a standing position at the top of the circle, players push the ball out in front of them in one long dribble, sprint behind the ball, catch it, and shoot the layup. The dribble should not be so high as to constitute an illegal dribble, of course, but it must be far enough in front of the dribbler to allow him to catch the ball inside the free-throw line. Otherwise, the dribbler's takeoff will be from the free-throw line or farther away from the basket, and he will have to throw the ball or take a jump shot rather than shoot a normal layup.

Variation: Two-Dribble Layup From the Wing. This variation may be performed from either sideline wing position, using two dribbles to get to the basket instead of one. The dribbles should be exaggerated slightly. The object is to teach young players to move the ball forward when dribbling at high speed instead of pushing every dribble straight down. The coach should not worry that his players will carry the ball in games as a result of practicing this drill: the skill is easily learned and needs only minimal practice to become a permanent part of every player's repertoire.

To vary the routine further, players may be lined up at the half-court line and instructed to shoot layups after taking two dribbles. Two-dribble layups from half-court require more exaggerated dribbling than other drills in this category, but they amply illustrate the problem involved in teaching youngsters to push the ball forward when dribbling at high speed instead of pushing every dribble straight down.

Chase

Although technically a conditioning drill, Chase also provides concentrated practice in all three aspects of high-speed layups: keeping the ball in front and ahead of one's body, knowing the whereabouts of the defensive player(s) while dribbling, and concentrating on the basket when the shot is taken.

Players line up in pairs out of bounds at one end of the court. The first player sets up behind the baseline corner with a ball, and his partner aligns himself on one side or the other as the defensive player. (See Figure 8–1.) The ballhandler starts whenever he wants, but the defensive player may not start until the ball hits the floor on the first dribble. The dribbler's objective is, of course, to make the layup at the other end of the court, though the defender will try

Figure 8–1   "Chase" Drill

to catch, turn, and control him before he reaches the basket. If the defender is successful, he and the dribbler will go one-on-one until a shot is taken. They switch responsibilities coming back downcourt.

If the defender steals the ball, he attempts to fast break and score at his end of the court. Play stops when either player takes a shot.

Players should be paired according to speed. Slower players or poorer ballhandlers may be allowed a step or two onto the court to equalize speed disadvantages.

Z Drill

If we were suddenly required to abandon all but one drill from our practices, we would have no trouble making our decision. The Z drill is, in our opinion, the most versatile drill in basketball. As a de-

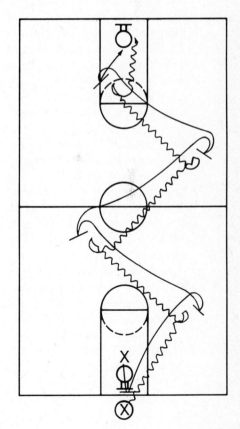

Figure 8–2 Z Drill

fensive drill, it can be used to stress positioning, overguarding, stopping (or controlling) the dribbler, and all the components of one-on-one basketball. From an offensive standpoint, the dribbler may be told to practice high-speed or protective dribbling, reverse pivoting, advancing the ball downcourt against pressure defense, or weakhand dribbling, depending upon the situation and coaching preferences.

The ballhandler holds the ball behind the baseline out of bounds at the middle of the court (Figure 8–2). (Actually, we split the court in half lengthwise in order to provide twice as much action in the same amount of time. However, we have shown the courtwide version to illustrate fully the skills involved.) The defensive player stands between the rectangular lane dividers, ready to react to the dribbler's movements. The dribbler may go to his right or left with the ball, either by running or sliding as he dribbles (whichever the coach stipulates). He continues in his original direction until stopped by the defensive player. (If not stopped, he continues downcourt and shoots a layup.) When stopped, usually somewhere along the sideline, he reverse pivots and continues dribbling downcourt diagonally in the other direction until the defender stops him again. Thus, the Z drill involves a series of diagonal movements downcourt, with both offensive and defensive players trying to gain an advantage over the other.

When players are unskilled either offensively or defensively, they should slide downcourt rather than run, at least, until they learn to control their performances. Once this point is reached, however, the Z drill's potential is endless. The coach may let the players free-lance downcourt, faking, sliding, turning and running in any manner they wish in an attempt to gain an advantage over the defender; stress weak-hand dribbling in order to improve overall dribbling efficiency; alternate between high-speed and protective dribbling with the same hand in order to practice changing speeds while dribbling; or any of countless other methods for changing speeds or directions while dribbling.

Variation: Z Drill as a Change-of-Speed Dribbling Drill. The Z drill may be used as a change-of-pace dribbling drill by alternating high-speed and protective dribbling, either with or without defense. (See Figure 8–3.)

From a standing position, the ballhandler dribbles two or three times sliding backwards, with his body turned away from the defensive player and the ball back near his rear foot, and then pivots and sprints forward for three dribbles, with exaggerated upper body lean and the ball ahead of him.

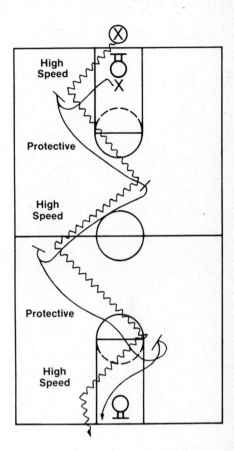

Figure 8–3   Z Drill as a Change-of-Speed Dribbling Drill

One-on-Two Drill

Like the Z drill, this drill serves the dual purpose of practicing offense and defense at the same time. Among other things, it can be used to recreate the double-teaming aspect of full-court pressing defense.

The one-on-two drill may be used to teach ballhandlers to recognize trapping movements and elude the double team as it improves their dribbling ability and sense of court presence. It also teaches defenders how to position themselves without losing control of the ballhandler in trapping situations.

In full-court pressing defenses, players are usually (but not always) single-guarded until they receive the inbounds pass. Therefore, in most cases, trapping involves one defender assuming cov-

Figure 8–4   One-on-Two Drill (*a*)

erage prior to another defender executing a trapping movement. Players can thus be taught to attack the double team sequentially.

As may be seen in Figures 8–4 through 8–7, X1 (player number 20) is the dribbler's first concern, since X1 will be the first defender to attempt to control the ballhandler. X1 will either move straight toward O1 (player number 14) (Figures 8–4 and 8–5), in which case, the dribbler should be able to drive around X1 along the sideline,

Figure 8–5   One-on-Two Drill (*b*)

Figure 8–6   One-on-Two Drill (*c*)

or to an overguarded position (Figures 8–6 and 8–7) in an effort to force X1 into the trapping defender.

Once defender X1 reaches a close or overguarded position, he is no longer an effective factor in tying up the dribbler or stealing the ball, especially if he is unable to force O1 to reverse pivot into X2 (player number 33). Instead of reverse pivoting, however, the dribbler should take one dribble toward X1 and, if X1 fails to over-guard him, sprint past him along the sideline using high-speed dribbling (Figures 8–4 and 8–5).

Figure 8–7   One-on-Two Drill (*d*)

Figure 8–8   One-on-Two Drill (*e*)

If, however, X1 slides to an overplaying position, O1 can take two quick left-handed dribbles to his left, switch to right-handed dribbling, and sprint past X2 so as to continue downcourt unmolested, thereby setting up a fast break for his team (Figures 8–6 and

Figure 8–9   One-on-Two Drill (*f*)

8–7). X2's natural impulse is to stop O1's movement to his left before stepping into position to stop O1's penetration between X1 and X2.

The dribbler's third alternative occurs when X2, like X1, overplays him toward the middle in order to force him to dribble with his left hand (Figures 8–8 and 8–9). If the ballhandler cannot dribble with his left hand, he will likely lose control of the ball trying to dribble downcourt at high speed. On the other hand, if O1 clears past X2, he will be able to switch back to right-handed dribbling and fast break without undue interference from X1 or X2.

In order to simulate game conditions as fully as possible in using the one-on-two drill, the coach might tell the defensive players to key their movements to the ballhandler's dribble and movements as follows: X1 moves into a close guarding position when the ballhandler says "Go!", but X2 cannot advance until the ballhandler begins dribbling. (Set X2 far enough apart from O1 to prohibit immediate double teaming.) If using this drill strictly for defensive purposes, the coach will set the defenders closer together. Constant repetition will familiarize the ballhandler with some of the trapping sequences he will face in games.

The same drill can be used on a half-court basis to practice trapping or controlling the dribbler or as an offensive drill to practice eluding defenders. In addition, the drill may be timed to determine how long the dribbler can elude the defenders and maintain ball possession or, conversely, to determine how long it takes the defenders to take the ball away. Appropriate rewards or punishment can be given for the best and/or worst performances. In setting up the drill, divide the players into groups of three, with players of equal speed within each group, and rotate the players every time their turn comes.

9

Rebounding Drills

Though height and natural jumping ability are contributing factors, when players consistently fail to block out aggressively or to position themselves so as to deny opponents easy access to rebounds, the chances are good that the coach did not stress rebounding techniques in practice.

Rebounding is based to a great extent on players' seeking out, and then maintaining, physical contact with their opponents. Shy or passive players must be taught to seek out this contact in order to block out effectively.

KINDS OF REBOUNDING DRILLS

Three-Man Rebounding

The three-man rebounding drill may be performed from either a triangular formation (Figure 9–1) or a straight-line formation (Figure 9–2). In either case, the defenders block out before going to the basket—and *they do not go directly to the basket*. Instead, they assume a position three to four feet away from the edge of the rim and attempt to keep their opponents behind them and away from the basket. The defenders should be taught to protect the ball after they land (knees bent, feet spread, elbows wide, and ball gripped solidly in both hands), and to turn toward the nearer sideline im-

Figure 9–1   Triangular Blocking
Formation

Figure 9–2   Straight-Line Rebounding Formation

Figure 9–3 Blocking Out (Circle) (*a*)

mediately and either dribble out of the crowd or pass to a teammate so as to begin fast breaking.

Blocking Out

In this drill, the ball is placed on the floor, with pairs of players circled around it facing each other. On signal, the offensive players

Figure 9–4 Blocking Out (Circle) (*b*)

on the outside of the circle try to reach the ball, and the defenders move to block them away from it. The drill may be timed so that one can determine which of the two teams can keep their opponents away from the ball for the longest time. This drill is designed to improve players' skills in moving to block opponents' paths to the basket in rebounding. Even more importantly, it makes players accustomed to the constant contact that effective rebounding requires and also provides practice in the cutting, sliding, and pivoting movements associated with rebounding. (See Figures 9–3 and 9–4.)

One-on-One Rebounding (From the Free-Throw Line)

Players line up on either side of the coach or a manager at the free-throw line or slightly in front of the free-throw line. When the coach shoots, the players at the front of each line move toward the basket to claim the rebound, with the rebounder becoming the offensive player and the other player assuming defensive coverage as they go one-on-one. (See Figure 9–5.)

Figure 9–5   One-on-One Rebounding Drill

This drill teaches players to rebound aggressively. More importantly, it teaches them to go back up with the ball after rebounding and provides additional practice in one-on-one basketball.

Five-on-Five Rebounding With Outlet Pass

The five-on-five rebounding drill is run the same as the three-man rebounding drill shown in Figure 9–1, except that it gives players the opportunity to practice checking opponents outside before going to the basket to rebound. In addition, after claiming rebounds, the team may set up its fast break by sending cutters into and along the passing lanes in whatever manner it deploys in game situations.

Rebounding Missed Free Throws

Setting players along the lane to rebound missed free throws provides good practice in both offensive and defensive rebounding. If two full teams of five players each are on the court, the defensive team may be able to practice fast breaking from missed free throws.

As far as the offense is concerned, the coach may want to have his players practice tipping rebounds out to teammates along the sideline if they aren't covered by defenders (Figure 9–6). Since only two offensive players are lined up along the lane (in addition to the shooter) against four defensive players, these men are more likely to tap the ball out to a teammate than to catch it and shoot it with the defenders in front and in back of them. As Figure 9–6 shows, O1, pinched between X1 and X3, elects to tip the ball out to O4 rather than risk catching the ball and being tied up by the defenders.

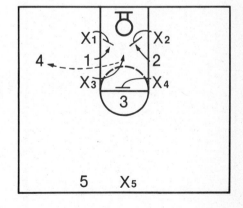

Figure 9–6 Rebounding Missed Free Throws (Tipping the Ball Outside)

(The opponents may elect to drop X3 back to cover O4, of course, but then O1 won't be harassed as much when he claims the offensive rebound.)

Junk Drill

As has been stated previously, weak outside shooters are more likely to overshoot (that is, shoot too hard) than to undershoot. Because of this tendency, an alert weak-side low-post offensive player in zone overload situations can "steal" a great many offensive rebounds for follow shots by blocking the defensive player in his area away from the weak side. Shots resulting from weak-side rebounding are called *junk* shots because they represent the leftovers from the offense that do not fall within the regular offensive shooting plan.

Most teams using zone defense "cheat" their players toward the ball side of the court when the ball is passed to the wing, in a manner similar to that shown in Figure 9–7. Such a defensive shift provides additional ball-side coverage and reduces the likelihood of undesirable matchups inside, especially X3's coverage of O4. If, for example, X3 stays back to cover O5, neither X1, X2 nor X4 will be able to drop back to help X5 when O4 is a superior one-on-one player inside. Therefore, X3 will usually shift toward the ball-side low post as shown to help out in the event of a lob pass when X3 is fronting O4.

The junk drill involves three players: an outside shooter at the wing (O2), an offensive player at the weak-side low post (O5) and a defensive player in the lane (X3).

Instead of going to the basket to rebound and thus allowing the weak-side defensive player access to the middle of the court, the

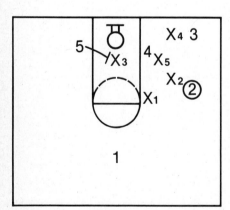

Figure 9–7 Blocking X5 Away from Weak Side for Offensive Rebounds

offensive player at the weak-side low post goes to the center of the lane to block out as the shot is taken. As a result, he is guaranteed weak-side rebounds on overshots. In addition, he has also reduced by 50 percent the defender's rebounding area in the middle of the court.

This simple maneuver is especially beneficial to teams with small players for whom offensive rebounds are the exception rather than the rule. Its proper execution can yield easy baskets as well as rebounds. Sometimes, of course, the weak-side defender will not leave low post. In such cases, the weak-side low-post offensive rebounder will have to work doubly hard to achieve a favorable rebounding position; yet he should be made aware that blocking out when opportunities arise will improve his chances of getting rebounds and scoring.

10

Shooting Drills

Great shooters are not developed during organized team practice. The finely coordinated movements involved in shooting a basketball are, for the most part, unnatural, and achieved only through countless hours of independent practice. We do, however, spend some practice time working on a variety of high-speed layups, since we expect our transition game to yield numerous layups off the press and in fast-break situations in the course of each game. In addition, we practice free throws increasingly as the season progresses, especially in simulated game conditions, since the players are usually unable to fabricate the pressure of a game on their own.

Great shooters are individuals who wanted to become outstanding players badly enough to practice shooting over a long period of time on their own. The coach's role in this process is to point out flaws in technique, suggest changes, and offer the players drills, games, and activities that enable them to practice their skills in their free time. (These same drills may be used in practice, of course.)

It is easier to become a great defensive player than a great shooter. Even if they're poor jumpers, weak ballhandlers, and erratic shooters, players can become superior defensively by hustling at practice, assuming and maintaining a low defensive stance, and learning overplaying techniques. However, no amount of hustle will teach them to put the ball through the hoop consistently. Shooting is an art involving finely coordinated small-muscle movements, which become habitual only as a result of long-term practice.

Some coaches place greater emphasis on shooting drills when they have good shooters than when they have weak shooters. With weak-shooting teams, they may spend most of their practice time working on defense and fast breaking and on improving ballhandling skills because they believe that they must compensate for the players' poor shooting abilities. A weak-shooting team, then, may be more likely to win because of its hard-nosed defense than because of its having a good shooting night. With such teams, good shooting will usually result from good shot selection and from ballhandlers who can get the ball to players in the clear.

SHOOTING DRILLS

Three-Man Shooting

This drill provides continuous movement, spot shooting with defense, and practice in following shots to the basket, the three essentials in offensive basketball. The player holding the ball under the basket passes and rushes toward the receiver to upset the receiver's concentration as he shoots. After shooting, the wing player follows his shot to the basket, rebounds, passes to the opposite wing player and moves toward him as before. The drill continues with each player in turn shooting, rebounding, passing, defending, and taking the shooter's place outside. (See Figures 10–1 through 10–4.)

Figure 10–1   Three-Man Shooting (a)

Figure 10–2 Three-Man Shooting (*b*)

Figure 10–3 Three-Man Shooting (*c*)

Figure 10–4 Three-Man Shooting (*d*)

Team Shooting

Players are divided into two or three groups of players aligned in single file at three different spots on the court. (The groups should be as equal in shooting skills as possible for maximum benefit.) On signal, the first player in each line shoots, follows his shot to the basket, and passes to the next player in line. He then moves to the rear of his line as the pass receiver shoots and recovers the ball in order to pass to the third player in line. Each team keeps score of the number of shots it has made, and when a designated number of successful field goals is reached, the game is over. Winners may be rewarded or losers penalized according to the coach's wishes. As in the three-man shooting drill, the positions from which shots are taken may be varied according to the coaches' wishes or team needs.

Two-Ball Inside Shooting

This drill provides continuous, intensive shooting practice at the low-post positions on either side of the lane. (See Figures 10–5 through 10–8.) One player holds the ball under the basket. As the designated shooter cuts to the low-post area, the ball is passed to a wing player, who relays the ball to the shooter. After the shot is taken, the ball is retrieved and passed to the wing player on the other side of the court. The shooter cuts back across the lane to ball-side low post and shoots on that side. The drill continues with all

Figure 10–5   Two-Ball (Inside) Shooting (a)

Figure 10–6 Two-Ball (Inside) Shooting (*b*)

Figure 10–7 Two-Ball (Inside) Shooting (*c*)

Figure 10–8 Two-Ball (Inside) Shooting (*d*)

shots rebounded and passed to the wings until the shooter has made a specific number of shots; then the four players rotate positions.

Horse

Possibly the oldest and best-known shooting game in basketball, horse is still popular today. The object of the game is to give opponents letters by making shots they cannot make in turn until the opposition has collected H–O–R–S–E and thus has been eliminated from the game.

Any number of players can participate, with the winner being the last player left in the game who has not received an E. When a player makes his shot, the next player has to make the same shot from the same area—a hook shot from the corner, for example—or else receive a letter. If the previous shooter missed his shot, the new player has a free turn, and may take any kind of shot he wishes from any place on the court.

Around the World

Like Horse, Around the World does not normally require dribbling or movement, but is purely a shooting competition. In Around the World, players are required to make a series of shots from predetermined areas, beginning at the basket and working their way around the perimeter of the court, with the winner being the first player to make shots from every position—or to go all the way around and back. If a player misses his shot, his turn is over, and he stays at that position until his next turn.

In one form of the game, players are allowed to take a second-chance shot if they miss their first shot from a given spot; however, if they miss the second shot, they have to return to the basket and start over on their next turn.

Putout

Putout is a mass shooting game somewhat similar to Horse. In Putout, however, everyone shoots the same shot from the same area, and instead of collecting letters, players are eliminated from the game if they miss a shot not missed by a previous player. (If the previous player missed his shot, the shooter does not have to make his shot to remain in the game.) The winner is the last player remaining who has not been "put out." Any number of participants can play; the more players there are, the better the game.

Because Putout eliminates weak shooters early in the game, it is not recommended for coaches hoping to improve all of their players' shooting skills. Yet, the game is popular among players of junior high age or below and can be a good drill to teach inexperienced players to concentrate on their shots, particularly layups.

Twenty-One

In its original form, Twenty-One was played by having each participant take three shots: from the top of the circle (three points if made), from wherever he got the rebound (two points), and a layup (one point). If he made all three shots, he was given another three-shot sequence and so on, until he either won the game by scoring twenty-one points or more or missed a shot. If he missed a shot, he would finish the sequence and then wait for his next turn. The variations were numerous: If a player finished his turn with exactly thirteen or eighteen points, his score went back to zero; if he scored more than twenty-one points, he had to start over; or if his shot failed to hit the backboard, basket, or rim, he either (1) was eliminated from the game, (2) had to go back to zero, or (3) lost the rest of his turn.

In the present-day form of Twenty-One, a player takes two shots, one from the free-throw line (two points if made) and a layup (one point). If he makes both shots, he continues to shoot in two-shot sequences until he either scores twenty-one or more points or misses a shot. If he misses a shot, he must wait his turn to shoot again.

Step Back

Step Back is from the same family of shooting games as Horse and Twenty-One. Although purely a shooting game, it does not involve dribbling, defensive coverage, or other aspects of competitive basketball. It may be used to teach younger players when to shoot for the backboard and when to aim at the rim. It can also be used to sharpen jump-shooting skills.

Though any number of players may participate, the game is most enjoyable and instructive with two or three players. Play begins with one player shooting from the free-throw line. If he makes the shot, he scores one point and takes one step backward to shoot again. As long as he makes his shots, he continues to step back and shoot; however, the first time he misses, the next player rebounds and shoots from wherever he gets the ball. He also scores a point for every successful shot and steps back one pace every time he scores.

If more than two players are involved in the game, the third player rebounds and shoots when the second player misses; however, if only two players are in the game, they take turns shooting. The game ends when one player scores twenty-five points, although that player continues shooting and scoring until he misses. At that point, every player in the game is allowed one more turn to catch him.

There are four optional rules in this game:

1. The player who shoots first also shoots last.
2. Whenever a player misses the rim and backboard entirely in shooting, the next player has the option of taking the ball back to the free-throw line.
3. Whenever another player besides the rebounder touches the ball, the rebounder may shoot from the point where the ball was touched if he wishes.
4. Any time a player makes five consecutive shots from beyond the free-throw line, he may return to the free-throw line. It should also be noted that players who step forward when they shoot should take *two* steps backward. In addition, the backward steps should be away from the basket in whichever direction the players faced when they rebounded the ball.

11

Defensive Drills

For organizational purposes, we've divided this chapter into three sections: stance, drills for guarding the ballhandler and receivers, and competitive drills.

STANCE

Let's now discuss some drills that can help to improve the defensive stance of players.

Step-Slide Drill

The success or failure of any defensive system in basketball depends to a large extent on the players' ability to assume, and then maintain, a sound defensive stance not only when stationary but also when moving in a variety of patterns. One of the best drills to teach players proper techniques of stance and movement is the step-slide drill. (See Figures 11–1 and 11–2.)

In the basic step-slide drill, the players line up along the sideline facing one end of the court. On command, they assume a wide, low defensive stance. (Some coaches have their players recite the elements of the basic defensive stance—"Feet spread, knees bent, tail down, back straight, and head and shoulders up!"—prior to beginning the step-slide movement.) Then, on a second command,

157

Figure 11–1   Step-Slide Drill (*a*)

they move across the court in unison, beginning with a step of no more than six to eight inches with their inside foot and following with a slide of no more than six to eight inches. Thus they cross the court slowly with a step-slide–step-slide cadence. Players may also be divided into "step" and "slide" groups. They clap and shout "Step!" on every step or "Slide!" on every slide as they move across the court. If anyone gets out of step—for example, by stepping while everyone else is sliding or vice versa—everyone has to go back to the sideline and start over.

Players do not ordinarily like step-sliding, particularly in the beginning stages of practice before they are in good shape. Assuming and maintaining a wide, low defensive stance, even without moving, can be painful. Maintaining such a stance for fifteen to thirty seconds at a time is difficult in the early stages. However, as players

Figure 11–2   Step-Slide Drill (*b*)

become accustomed to doing this through daily practice, the soreness soon goes away.

Players do not need to maintain this kind of defensive stance throughout games; however, they should be able to assume and maintain an effective defensive stance whenever the need arises and for as long as necessary to provide effective defensive coverage (for example, when influencing the dribbler or cutting off the perimeter passing lanes). Because most players will not naturally assume and maintain the kind of defensive stance we're talking about here, they must be *trained* to do so. The step-slide drill provides an excellent means for achieving this end.

In executing the step-slide movement, players often commit three major errors that limit the effectiveness of their defensive maneuverability: (1) standing up (not bending the knees or getting the tail down), (2) permitting the knees to come together in the "slide" segment, and (3) taking large steps. One good way of dealing with these problems is to have the player assume a defensive stance while placing a broomstick behind his knees and holding it with his hands positioned between his knees in front of him. His hands should be held as far apart as his knees will permit, and his knees should not be permitted to come any closer as he steps and slides across the court than they would be in the stationary defensive stance.

Variation: The most popular variation of the step-slide drill involves step-sliding diagonally backward for a prescribed distance or time—say, three "steps" and two "slides"—and then dropping the outside, or "slide," foot back to change direction. The angle of drop step establishes the direction of the defender's movement and also establishes his original "slide" foot as his new "step" foot. For example, a player might *step* to his left with his left foot, *slide* with his right foot, *step* with his left foot, and *drop* his right foot back to reverse the direction of his diagonal retreat to his right. Then he might *slide* his left foot prior to stepping again with his left foot.

In using the drop-step/diagonal step-slide, the coach should remember that the players' physical tolerance for an effective defensive stance is limited by their physical conditioning and can be built up from, say, fifteen-second segments to upwards of a minute.

Wave Drill (Defensive)

Players line up in rows of three or four at one end of the court facing the coach at midcourt. On the command "Set" they assume a defensive stance. On the command "Go," they begin sliding forward in their stance and change direction whenever the coach points in a given direction. We recommend starting players off with fifteen-second periods of movement and building their endurance gradually until they are capable of moving in their stance for forty-five to sixty seconds at a time.

Unlike in the step-slide drill where players move slowly, here they should be urged to move as quickly as possible, since the real value of the wave drill lies in reducing defensive reaction time.

Denying the Inside Pass

This simple drill is excellent for teaching players to maintain effective defensive positioning in denying passes inside the lane or to low post. It requires three offensive players at the point and wing positions and a low-post player and defender inside. The drill begins with the ball at one wing and the defender overguarding to deny the pass to low post on that side of the court. The ballhandler can pass to either of the two other players outside or to the post if the defender isn't overguarding adequately. The post man can go anywhere he wishes to receive a pass from any of the three perimeter players except beyond the nearer boundary of the free-throw circle in the lane. (The object of the drill is to teach players how to overguard the passing lane and to avoid being beaten by lob passes when the post man cuts to the basket from high post.) High-post coverage is best taught as part of a team defense, with at least three, and preferably four or five, defenders participating.

Monkey Drill

The monkey drill is really not a drill for improving stance but rather one for conditioning players' legs for the defensive stance. Players line up along the sideline or baseline facing the center of the court with their feet wide and their center of gravity low. On command, they begin shuffling along the line, slapping the floor with their palms (or touching the floor with their fingertips if they're sufficiently out of shape) on every shuffling movement for as many laps as the coach deems necessary.

Because the monkey drill can be performed more quickly than the step-slide drill and with less constant supervision, it is best used as a punishment (for example, for habitual lateness, absence from practice, or low grades) rather than for building defensive skills. It's just too easy to keep the legs relatively straight and bend the back in touching the floor.

DRILLS FOR GUARDING THE BALLHANDLER AND RECEIVERS

Bluff and Run

Although the term *picking up the dribbler* can refer to full-court pressing or half-court defense, we are using it in the sense of "assuming defensive coverage of any ballhandler who was previously unguarded," especially as he moves downcourt at any given point. Picking up and then controlling a moving ballhandler, particularly when he is moving directly at the defender, ranks among the most difficult skills in basketball to acquire.

The defender may elect either to stand still and wait for the ballhandler to come to him or to move toward the ball in an effort to use his forward momentum to gain defensive control of the dribbler. Believing that *action* is superior to *reaction* in terms of achieving and maintaining defensive control, we naturally favor the latter technique. We don't like the idea of waiting for somebody to bring the attack to us. In most cases, the advantages lie with the attacking team.

Still, we're not talking about a wild rush toward the ballhandler. Rushing is the easiest way to guarantee that you'll *never* control the dribbler: he'll go around the defender like water through a screen door. We drill our players constantly in picking up the ballhandler, beginning with the first day of practice and working at this skill constantly in our practices until they learn to do it properly. Though even the good defenders get beaten regularly in the earliest stages of practice, they eventually meet with success. Then we teach them such plays as drawing the charging foul and influencing the dribbler in a given direction.

We employ a technique called *bluff and run.** Using a series of fake steps, the defender will alternately retreat from, and move toward, the dribbler so as to keep him off-balance as he (the defender) gradually closes the distance between them. (In games, teammates away from the ball will also "bluff" toward the dribbler occasionally, as if double teaming or trapping; in early practice, however, we want the defender to learn to do this by himself, without having to depend on his teammates.)

In practicing bluff-and-run drill, we use a split-court technique on a one-on-one basis (Figure 11–3), with the guards and small

* For more in-depth information concerning bluff and run and other techniques of pressure man-to-man defense, see our book *Winning Basketball Systems* (Boston: Allyn and Bacon, Inc., 1981).

Figure 11–3 Bluff-and-Run Drill

forwards on one side of the court and the centers and tall forwards on the other side of the court.

Later, we add a defender downcourt beyond the ballhandler (Figure 11–4), who retreats and fakes toward the ball. Still later, we add a second defender downcourt, who also retreats and fakes. Bluff-and-run movements away from the ball divert the ballhandler's attention and reduce his attacking potential. If he concentrates only on the player guarding him, he can be double teamed and if he has to watch the other defenders, he is far more easy to pick up and control defensively.

Z Drill

Picking up the dribbler is the first step in controlling the ballhandler. The second step is directing his movements toward an area of the court that does not increase the offense's scoring capabilities.

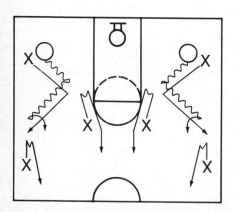

Figure 11–4 Bluff-and-Run Drill with a Second Defender

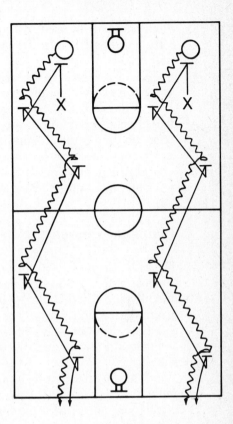

Figure 11–5 Z Drill Used to
Teach Pressure Defensive Control

In some cases, influencing the dribbler means using superior defensive skills to keep him outside and to make him pick up the ball; in other cases, it means forcing his dribble in a prearranged direction or toward a predetermined area of the court.

On a full-court basis, the best drill for teaching how to influence the dribbler is the Z drill. (See Figure 11–5.) It is also superb for teaching such defensive techniques as turning the dribbler and forcing weak-hand dribbling.

In using the Z drill on a full-court basis, we suggest using the split-court technique, with guards and small forwards paired up on one side of the court and centers and tall forwards on the other side. In running the Z drill as a defensive drill, the dribbler should be instructed not to change directions until he is completely stopped at the sideline by the defender and not to use fakes to gain offensive control—at least, in early preseason practice. During this period, the defender should be able to concentrate on cutting his man off at the sideline and overguarding him to influence weak-hand dribbling, without having to react to fakes. Later, as skills increase (or when the drill is used to improve offensive skills), the coach may permit the ballhandler to use free-lance moves and fakes in the Z drill.

A useful way of stressing the value of body positioning and using "quick feet" on defense is to have the defenders hold a towel in both hands behind their backs as they work their man in the Z drill. Because beginners are likely to guard their men with their arms, holding a towel behind their backs can help teach them how to use their feet and bodies to control ballhandlers.

Our drills for controlling the dribbler on a half-court basis are described in Chapter 16 as well as in *Winning Basketball Systems.*

Taking the Charge

The Z drill is also ideal for teaching players to draw charging fouls (for example, by faking a move toward the ball and then stepping quickly into the dribbler's path as he spin-dribbles away from his original direction) and to take the charge with minimal risk to life and limb. The offensive player can be told (either with or without the defender's knowledge) "Don't stop when he cuts you off at the sideline."

Taking the charge is an indispensable part of each player's individual defense. We work on this technique constantly, and give a trophy at our awards banquet every year to the player who takes the most charges in games. You cannot be a complete defensive player if you will not take the charge.

Other game situations conducive to taking the charge can be drilled: for example, having a pivot man step out into a cutter's path in splitting the high post; cutting off the baseline drive; or moving into the ballhandler's path in defensing a two-on-one fast break.

Covering the Fast Break

In covering a one-on-one fast break, it is important that players learn not to foul needlessly—for example, when the player is obviously going to make the shot, and fouling him would only give him a chance to make three points on the play instead of two. In an era in which blocked shots are treated with reverence by players and fans alike, it is more important to teach players when *not* to foul than when to foul.

Layups, and their defense, should be practiced from all angles, including those in which the likelihood of fouling is great enough

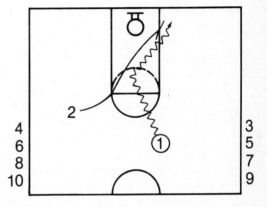

Figure 11–6 Pressuring the
Shooter (Layups)

to discourage trying to block the shot altogether (for example, reaching across the ballhandler's body from the left to block a right-handed shot). In addition to explaining this drill so as to learn when and when not to attempt to block shots, defenders should use it to practice cutting off the dribbler, drawing the charging foul, and running through the dribbler's path as he picks up his dribble in order to try to steal the ball. (See Figure 11–6.)

In operating the drill, the first player in line at a given area of the court attempts to cut off the other player's route to the basket and force him to pick up his dribble prematurely in an attempt to reduce the offensive player's attacking advantage. After the confrontation, the offensive player moves to the back of the defensive line, and the defensive player goes to the back of the offensive line.

Players should also be drilled in defensing two-on-one fast breaks. Players line up in two rows at or beyond the top of the circle, with a defender in the lane facing them. The first players in each line break toward the basket, either dribbling or passing the ball between them. The defender tries to disrupt the play and/or prevent the layup. The defenders should be changed every ten to twelve attempts until everyone has had a chance to play defense.

The coach can make the drill more competitive by having players keep individual scores as follows: on defense, a player gets *one* point for a missed shot and two points for a steal or blocked shot. On offense, players get two points for a made shot (they're only allowed one shot, and that shot must come directly off the fast break) and no points for a missed shot. Players accumulate points until everyone has completed his allotted number of defensive trials. The winner is the player with the highest aggregate point total.

Teams should also practice three-on-two, three-on-three, four-on-three, four-on-four, and five-on-four fast-break defense. As with the two-on-one drills, individual scores can be kept to make the drill more competitive.

In defensing three-on-two fast breaks, we prefer a one-up, one-back alignment (as opposed to a side-by-side arrangement). The outside defender stationed at the free-throw line is responsible for stopping the ballhandler's advance and making him pick up his dribble and then in dropping back to cover the lane and basket area opposite the pass. The inside defender covers the pass receiver, cuts off his route to the basket, and tries to hinder the inside pass to the other wing cutter.

The most important element in drilling fast-break defense in situations featuring offensive numerical superiority (for example, three-on-two, two-on-one, and so on) is teaching the defender(s) to use fakes and a variety of coverages to force the ballhandler into mistakes such as picking up the ball too far from the basket, committing a turnover or charging foul, or maneuvering himself into a position where his passing options are sharply reduced if not completely eliminated. When the defender is able to use fake steps toward the ball to conceal his true intentions without appreciably altering his own court position, he creates pressure on the dribbler to make correct decisions while traveling at high speed. In many cases, the dribbler will slow down enough to allow additional defenders to move into position to offset the offense's numerical superiority.

The defender(s) need not attack the fast-breaking players to upset their offensive advantage, but they must be able to give the *appearance* of making attacking movements. The *worst* thing defenders can do is to attack the fast break away from the basket area, at half court, for example. This action gives the offense an unimpeded route to the basket if the offense eludes the coverage, or if the defenders retreat to the basket and wait passively for the offense to attack, relying on nothing more than defensive reaction to stop the fast break.

As far as alignments are concerned, we prefer a single defender covering the ball—that is, a one-up, two-back alignment in covering four-on-three fast breaks (as opposed to a two-up, one-back alignment that would permit the offense to split the defensive coverage with a ballhandler, two wings, and trailer).

Two-on-One Passing Drill

One drill used in teaching players to deny perimeter passes is the two-on-one passing drill. Two offensive players face each other across the free-throw lane (or at the wing position, at the high or low post, or wherever the coach wants to set them) with a single defender between them. The defender is permitted to move into a close guarding position on the ballhandler. On command the ball-handler tries to pass to his teammate, and the defender tries to deflect the pass or force the ballhandler into making an inaccurate pass. If the drill is performed along the free-throw lane, the defender is given time to move into position so as to guard the other player before the drill is repeated. The defender may be coached to use a one-hand-at-the-ball,   one-hand-in-the-most-likely-alternate-pass-ing-lane stance (for example, with the ball held low on the ball-handler's right side, the defender's left hand would be low and near the ball to deny the bounce pass and his right hand would be raised to deny the direct pass if the ballhandler suddenly brings the ball up). When the ballhandler holds the ball above or behind his head, the defender may place both hands above his head in denying the pass. In either case, the important thing is to give the defender time to move into a close-guarding stance before allowing the ballhandler to pass the ball.

In our pressure man-to-man defensive drills, we stress pressuring the passer and playing one step off the line of the ball and the receiver and two steps toward the ball. Thus, we practice perimeter pass denial (at least, concerning the primary passing lanes) in all our drills and controlled scrimmaging sequences. The two most important aspects of pressure man-to-man defense are (1) constant, intense pressure on the ball and (2) the denial of passes to the posts and primary pass receivers along the perimeter. We use two-on-two, three-on-three, four-on-four, and five-on-five drills and controlled scrimmaging to practice on-the-ball pressure and pass denial from every conceivable part of the half and full court. (We also work our players hard on switching quickly from on-the-ball defense to pass denial, and vice versa.)

Cutting Off the Baseline Drive

If our on-the-ball defense is performed properly and defenders one pass away from the ball are cutting off the primary passing lanes, the ballhandler is forced toward the sideline, and then the baseline, from an exaggerated overguarded defensive stance. In such cases, it is imperative that our players be able to establish a cutoff point, retreat to beat their men to that point, and regain defensive control. While we do not, and cannot, expect defenders to beat their men to the cutoff point every time, we expect them to try.

Our sideline-influence defense permits us to practice this skill every time the ball is put into play in drills or controlled scrim-

Figure 11–7   Defensing the Baseline Drive

maging. (Our cutoff points are [1] the ten-second mark at the sideline, [2] the baseline corner, and [3] the baseline three feet outside the lane.) Of course, we want to influence the ballhandler toward the first cutoff point, but if that fails, we want him to try to catch his man in time to steer him toward the second cutoff point, and so on. This technique is described in greater detail in *Winning Basketball Systems.*

For coaches who do not use sideline-influence techniques but still want to teach their players to cut off the baseline drive, we suggest a simple drill along the sideline, as shown in Figure 11–7.

The ballhandler and his defender stand along the sideline, with the ballhandler facing the baseline and the defender facing his man. On command, the ballhandler dribbles toward the sideline. As his defender pivots, the ballhandler attempts to beat him to the prearranged cutoff point before he can pivot back into his defensive stance facing the dribbler. In the early stages of practice, the dribbler might be instructed to dribble around a chair placed on the court near the corner in order to minimize the defender's disadvantage until he learns to react quickly to the dribbler's movements. Later, the chair can be removed, and the drill can be extended to include the dribbler and defender going one-on-one from the corner when the defender successfully cuts his man off.

Figure 11–8   One-on-One Drill (With Coach)

COMPETITIVE DRILLS

One-on-One Drills

One-on-one situations are the backbone of basketball. All basketball, whether zone or man-to-man, eventually resolves into one-on-one confrontations; therefore the coach should teach his players to handle one-on-one matchups at least adequately. Countless drills, such as the Z drill, can be used to accomplish this goal. In the present context, however, we're considering drills in which, if the defender fails, his man is likely to score against him.

One fine full-court one-on-one drill places a player on either side of the coach along the baseline. (See Figure 11–8.) The coach rolls or throws the ball downcourt, and the two players race toward the ball. The player who gets to the ball first becomes the offensive player, and the other player becomes the defender as they play one-on-one back downcourt. Only one shot is allowed at either end. If the defender is able to steal the ball without fouling, he fast breaks to the other end of the court and shoots the lay-up. If stopped, he goes one-on-one at that end of the court.

In this drill, players of approximately equal speed should be paired. If not, the same player will become the offensive player every time. (This problem can be eliminated by giving the slower player a head start or by rolling or throwing the ball toward the slower player's side of the court.)

The same drill can be done on a "team" basis from midcourt by dividing the squad into two teams and giving each player a number corresponding to that of a player on the other team. The two groups stand out of bounds on either side of the court. The ball is placed in the free-throw circle, and the coach calls out a given number, say, "Five!" When their number is called out, the two *five* players race toward the ball. The one who reaches it first drives toward his basket, and the other player tries desperately to stop him. Whichever "team" scores receives two points, and the two players return to their sidelines to wait for another number to be called. A player who is fouled receives two free throws, after which both players return to the sideline regardless of whether the player receiving the free throw made either or both shots.

This drill adapts well as a two-, three-, four- or five-player drill. The only danger involved is that two players might run together or crack heads while reaching for the ball.

Adding a coach or manager to one-on-one drills can broaden the objectives. For example, in half-court one-on-one situations, allowing the offensive player to pass to the coach whenever he wishes permits the defender to practice pass denial coverage as well as the on-the-ball coverage he obtains from regular one-on-one drills.

One-on-Two Drill

One further aspect of team defense involving a single defender and two offensive players remains to be discussed: the help-and-recover technique. When the ballhandler is able to elude his man and drive toward the basket, team defense dictates that he must be picked up by another defender; he cannot be allowed to shoot an unmolested layup. Still, in most cases, the amount of time necessary for the defender to catch his man is usually minimal. Thus a switching defender does not have to assume complete control of the driver but needs merely to slow him up or delay his progress until his defender catches up with the play.

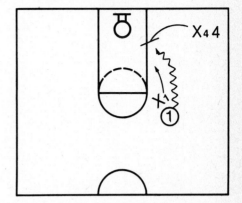

Figure 11–9 Switching Off to
Defend Against Drives

    In Figure 11–9, the defender is guarding his man rather closely in the corner. As the ballhandler at the wing advances toward the basket, the offensive corner player moves toward the basket. The defender, sliding at first with his man, steps out to stop the dribbler; then, as the dribbler picks up the ball, the defender retreats quickly to recover his original man. Players rotate in the drill from defense to ballhandler at the wing to the back of the line in the corner.

    In the earliest stages of using this drill we suggest going through it at half speed and keeping the angle between the offensive players rather acute. Later, as defenders become more adept at helping out and recovering, the drill can be speeded up and the angle increased to, say, the corner and top of the circle.

III

Team Drills

12

Fast-Breaking Drills

All full-court running drills condition players for fast breaking. However, they do not necessarily drill players in high-speed ball-handling, cutting into or following passing lanes downcourt, or taking advantage of offensive superiority at the end of the fast break.

GENERAL CONSIDERATIONS FOR LEADING THE FAST BREAK

1. Center the ball as quickly as is feasible. Use high-speed dribbling (or pass downcourt) to move the ball beyond the first level of defense. Exceptions do exist, but generally the ball should be taken down the middle of the court, where the passing angles spread the defense to the maximum.

2. Don't force the ball downcourt by dribbling, particularly if you are unprepared to deal with sudden double teams.

3. Pass to open teammates downcourt ahead of the ball. Passing, even a series of passes, is always the fastest way to move the ball downcourt (although not necessarily the *safest* method).

4. Make the pass when it should be made, not when it looks best. The temptation always exists to take a few more dribbles than necessary, since everybody in the stands is watching the player with the ball. The truly effective ballhandler takes only as many dribbles as are necessary to gain control of the ball and to find an open

teammate ahead of him. This may mean taking one dribble and passing the ball or taking the ball all the way to the basket himself.

5. Don't force passes. If your teammates are covered, don't attempt to pass the ball. (Young players should be discouraged from attempting long passes downcourt to open teammates beyond their passing range. Instead, they should be taught to dribble downcourt until they reach a point where they can reach their teammates with a pass.)

If no one is open at the end of the break, try to set up your own shot, look for a teammate trailing the play, or take the ball back outside and set up in your half-court offense.

6. Use the pass with the greatest chance of succeeding. A bounce pass or chest pass may not stir up the fans as much as a leaping, twisting, pump-fake or behind-the-back pass, but a pass doesn't have to be fancy to be effective.

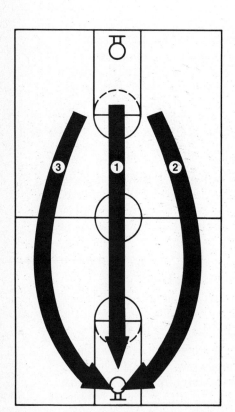

Figure 12–1 "Laning" the Three-Man Fast Break

7. Control the dribble prior to passing the ball. A ballhandler is controlling his dribble when he can look up to see where he is going and find his teammates and the opponents in the process, without endangering the possession of the ball.

8. Don't challenge a defender at the end of the fast break if you're not prepared to deal with his response.

9. If you are left unguarded at the end of the break, drive down the middle for the layup or take the shot from the free-throw line. All successful fast breaks are based on getting the ball to the open man, and the open man should always be prepared to take the shot.

10. Look for trailers if the initial fast break fails. When the opponents can get three defenders back to cover your three fast-breaking men, an offensive player trailing the break can swing the advantage back to the fast-breaking team.

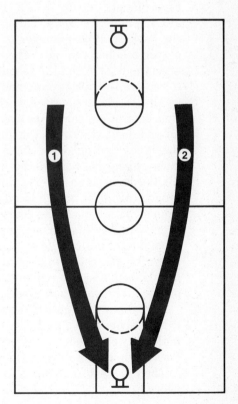

Figure 12–2 "Laning" the Two-Man Fast Break

SETTING UP THE FAST BREAK

In setting up the fast break once transition has occurred, the coach may choose either to (1) "lane" the break by assigning lanes to specific players (for example, the ballhandler in lane 2 in Figure 12–1 and Lane 1 in Figure 12–2) or (2) permit players to free-lance downcourt as long as they fill the lanes. No claim is made at this point for the superiority of either system, but the coach must specify which system is to be used in drills.

Although there are countless drills for setting up and running the fast break, we use only two in our early preseason practices, the five-player (one-minute) fast-break drill and the eleven-player fast-break drill. (Later, we practice fast breaking from controlled scrimmage situations, as described in Chapter 16.)

The Five-Player (One-Minute) Fast-Break Drill

Five players set up in a 2–1–2 (or 1–3–1 or 1–2–2, and so on) alignment on the court. The coach stands at the free-throw line with the basketball. A manager is ready to start the clock as soon as a player touches the ball. The coach shoots, and the rebounders go after the ball. When the rebound is taken, the ballhandler(s) moves to receive the outlet pass, and other players fill the wing positions as all five players start downcourt. They shoot at the other end and then fast break the other way in the same fashion. They continue up and down the court, rebounding, making the outlet pass, filling the lanes and shooting, for a full minute, keeping score of shots made. Regardless of whether the same players handle the ball and fill the same lanes every time downcourt or use a free-lance approach, all players should go at least to the free-throw line every time at both ends of the court.

A highly disciplined approach is to use the same players as rebounders, ballhandlers, and cutters at both ends of the court. However, the coach may prefer to use a free-lance approach to the laning assignments and cuts, especially if he has players with approximately equal ballhandling skills.

A team with good-to-outstanding speed may make thirteen to fifteen shots in a minute; a team with average speed may make none to twelve shots in one minute. Scoring high in the five-player fast-break drill requires good ballhandling, attention to wide laning in the process of moving downcourt, and concentration in shooting every layup.

Eleven-Player Fast-Break Drill

As might be expected, this drill requires at least eleven players. The starting positions for this drill, which provides constant motion and practice in both fast breaking and defensing fast breaks, are shown in Figure 12–3.

This eleven-player drill sets up continuous three-on-two fast breaks as follows: O1, O2, and O3 begin at midcourt, fast breaking against O4 and O5 on defense. O8 and O9 step onto the court, ready to fast break the other way with whomever claims the rebound. Say O4 rebounds, as shown in Figure 12–4. O4 passes to O9 on his side of the court and cuts down that sideline. O8 fills the passing lane on his side of the court as O9 takes the ball to the middle and downcourt, where O6 and O7 wait to play defense. (After O4, O8, and O9 leave, O5 moves to the back of a sideline line, and any two of the original three fast-breaking players fill the defensive positions at that end of the court.)

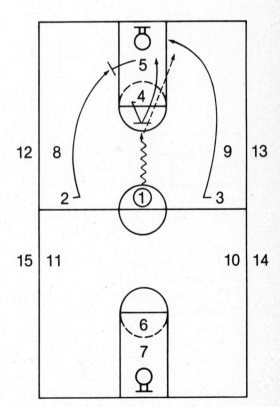

Figure 12–3 Starting the Eleven-Man Fast-Break Drill

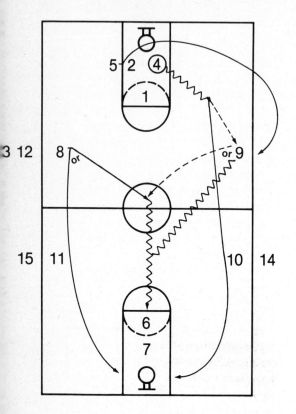

Figure 12–4 Continuing the Eleven-Man Fast-Break Drill

Any time a defensive player steals the ball, he immediately initiates the fast break going the other way with the next two players along the sideline. Players are allowed only one shot at the basket.

The drill may be continued for as long as desired with players continuously moving in and out of the fast break and defense. (The drill may degenerate into a series of ballhandling errors and turnovers unless players are urged to get the ball to the best ballhandler among the three.)

One variation that heightens interest in the drill is to have players keep individual scores as follows: when they successfully defend against the fast break, they score one point, and when they participate in a successful fast break, they score two points, regardless of whether they were the shooters.

Variation: Six-Player Fast-Break Drill. This drill is a variation of the eleven-player drill. The differences are that the fast break consists of continuous two-on-one breaks rather than three-

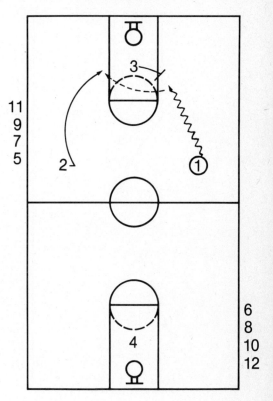

Figure 12–5 Starting the Six-Man Fast-Break Drill

on-two breaks and the outlet pass receivers are found on only one side of the court at each end. (See Figures 12–5 and 12–6.)

O1 and O2 begin by fast breaking against O3. Whoever claims the rebound (O1 in Figure 12–6) passes to O5, who by now has stepped onto the court along the sideline. They proceed downcourt two-on-one against O4. The rebounder at that end will then pass to O6 along the sideline to continue the drill in the other direction.

FINISHING THE FAST BREAK

Though drilling players in three-on-two fast breaking is important, the skills involved may be beyond the capabilities of unskilled ball-handlers. Since only one pass and one defender are involved, drilling players in two-on-one fast-break situations is far more satisfying in terms of positive short-term results. A coach is likely to be more successful starting with two-on-one fast breaking and progressing

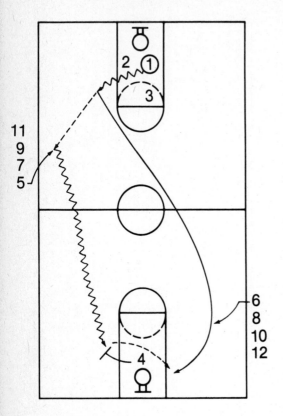

Figure 12–6 Continuing the Six-Man Fast-Break Drill

to three-on-two fast breaking as skills increase. (We're not saying don't practice three-on-two fast-break drills; however, coaches whose players make the ball seem like a cardboard box when dribbling probably should emphasize the two-on-one drill rather than the three-on-two drill in the earliest stages of practice.)

Three-on-Two Drill

Two players are selected to play defense with the rest of the team moving into three lines at half court. The same players defend against a specified number of three-man fast breaks, then move into the fast-breaking positions as two new men play defense. Only one shot is permitted, and no more than two passes may be made before shooting. (Baskets made after the third pass do not count.)

Scoring is as follows: Every player keeps his own score, and when the offensive team fails to score, both defenders receive one point. When the fast break results in a basket for the offense, all three players add one point to their scores. The game continues until all players have played defense for an allotted number of trials, at which time the players announce their scores. The winner receives some kind of reward for his efforts—for example, reduced sprints at the end of practice.

Two-on-One Drill

This drill is run exactly like the three-on-two drill except that only two offensive players and one defender participate at a time. Most coaches use twelve to fifteen fast-break attempts per defender to provide adequate defensive practice.

An interesting variation for players tired of practicing the two-on-one drill is to run the drill the same way as before (changing the defender every ten fast break attempts) but to permit the players to keep individual scores. Only one shot is allowed, and both offensive players get two points if they score. However, if they miss their shot, the defender gets one point, and if they fail to get a shot at all, whether by throwing the ball away or having the defender steal the ball, the defender gets two points. (Only layups count; players cannot pull up for jump shots.) The game is over when everyone has taken his turn as defender.

13

Beating the Press

In preparing his basketball team for competition, a coach's first tactical priority should be to devise methods for dealing with opponents' pressing defenses. Players must be instructed and drilled in specific techniques designed to advance the ball beyond the opponents' presses. Failure in this regard may result in games played largely in the opponents' offensive half court. Teams seldom score from their opponents' end of the court.

TWO-ON-ONE DRILL

The ballhandler can be trapped from a zone pressing alignment in two ways: by simultaneous trapping, that is, two or more defensive players arrive at the trapping site at the same time, or by delay trapping, that is, first one, then another defensive player arrives at the trapping site. In the case of simultaneous trapping, the ballhandler's only dribbling routes are likely to be along the sidelines. (See Figures 13–1 and 13–2, 13–5 and 13–6.) The other dribbling route, between the two defenders, is shown in Figures 13–3 and 13–4. Because we dislike simultaneous trapping used against us, we cut our ballhandler away from the trapping defenders in receiving the inbounds pass so to delay the trapping movement by the second guard. The pass receiver does not dribble past the double

185

Figure 13–1   Two-on-One Drill
(*a*)

Figure 13–2   Two-on-One Drill
(*b*)

Figure 13–3   Two-on-One Drill
(*c*)

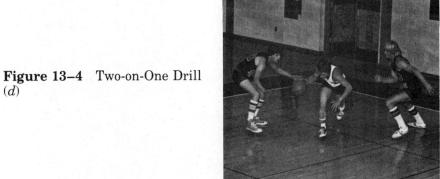

Figure 13–4   Two-on-One Drill (*d*)

Figure 13–5   Two-on-One Drill (*e*)

Figure 13–6   Two-on-One Drill (*f*)

Figure 13–7   Forcing a Double Team from Two-on-One (*a*)

team but turns and passes downcourt or waits for the inbounds passer to clear and then passes to him or the safety valve.

When one of the defenders either chooses, or is forced, to delay his trapping, the ballhandler's chances of dribbling downcourt are improved. Instead of dribbling around the trapping guards, he may be able to dribble *through* the trap or between the trapping guards.

In Figures 13–7 and 13–8, the outside defender attempts to trap the ballhandler immediately after he receives the inbounds pass. The ballhandler dribbles once or twice diagonally to his left, freezing the inside defender into deeper coverage. Suddenly, the ballhandler switches to dribbling with his right hand and cuts into the gap between the defenders.

Figure 13–8   Forcing a Double Team from Two-on-One (*b*)

"BEATING THE PRESS"

It is possible to practice your full-court press and beating the press at the same time by setting up your five starters to beat the press and by positioning your defensive players at various positions on the court to press the starters. Score is kept, using the following rules: if the offensive team gets the ball across the half-court line legally without losing the ball, it receives one point. It is allowed no more than one shot at the basket which, if successful, gives the team two more points. All fouls count one point for the opponents.

On the other hand, the defensive team receives one point for stealing the ball or forcing a turnover or ten-second backcourt violation. It is also allowed one shot after gaining possession of the ball and fast breaking.

In order to provide more intensive practice for the starters, you can put seven to nine defensive players on the court. This arrangement keeps the score close regardless of the superiority of your starters, makes the offensive players work harder, and forces them to concentrate for extended periods without relaxing.

14

Moving Game Drills

When I was coaching at Riverside City College, Pasadena City College and Long Beach State, we had two basic offensive styles, our *inside power game* and our *moving game.** Our moving game was similar to today's passing game offenses—that is, player movements were both free form and structured and designed to create and exploit option situations. For instance, a player passing the ball to a teammate had several options available: he could screen for the receiver, cut to the basket, or screen for a weak-side player. The subsequent actions of his teammates were dependent to a certain extent upon what he did. Then, as the receiver recognized what was developing, *he* had several options available to him (for example, driving, working his man one-on-one, or passing to a cutter) based upon his own court position, his teammates' movements, and so on. Movements were structured only insofar as was necessary to maintain court balance, such as filling positions vacated by cutters, or cutting or sliding into ball-side post areas.

We felt that this style of play gave our players more leeway to attack opponents than conventional patterns. The unpredictability of our patternless offensive style meant that opponents could not react automatically to our movements as they might against set plays or continuity patterns.

* See our book *Winning Basketball Systems* (Boston: Allyn and Bacon, Inc., 1981).

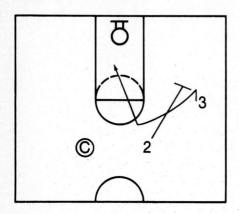

Figure 14–1   Guard-Forward Screen

The drills illustrated in Chapters 14 and 15 teach players to recognize the kinds of movement patterns available to them from various court positions. They should be practiced without defense at first, until the players become familiar enough with the sequences to add defenders.

GUARD–FORWARD PASS

Emphasis: (1) Set up defense to receive a pick and hold until the picker gets to your man, (2) vacate position on one count if you do not receive the ball, and (3) backdoor to the basket on all overplays. (See Figure 14–1.)
Emphasis: (1) The guard fills the farthest point away from the ball side of the floor, and (2) floor space is created for the forward to drive for a shot or hit the open man. (See Figure 14–2.)

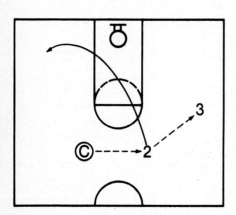

Figure 14–2   Guard-Forward Pass

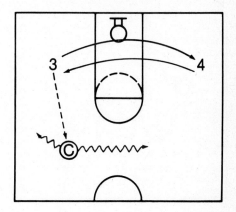

Figure 14–3 Forward-Guard Pass

FORWARD–GUARD PASS

Emphasis: Forward backdoors all overplays and clears to the other side of the court. (See Figure 14–3.)

Emphasis: The weak-side forward comes to the ball by either accepting the pick or refusing it and going under to post position. (See Figure 14–4.)

Emphasis: (1) Forward passes to guard and sets a rear pick or clears, and (2) guard penetrates and hits the open man. (See Figure 14–5.)

Emphasis: (1) Vacate position on one count if you do not receive the ball, and (2) backdoor all overplays. (See Figure 14–6.)

Emphasis: (1) Guard-guard pass keys the initiator of the pass to post up, and (2) if you post and do not get the ball, you step out

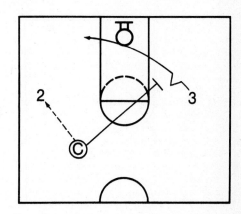

Figure 14–4 Weak-Side Screen

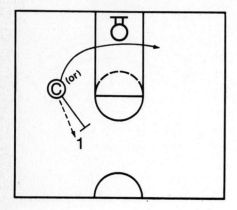

Figure 14–5   Pass and Move

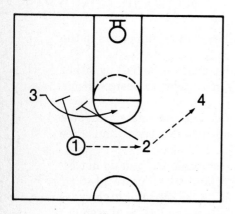

Figure 14–6   Pass and Screen

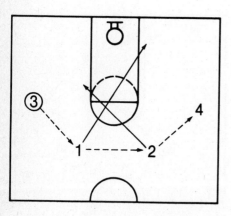

Figure 14–7   Pass and Post Up

and become a forward on the same side of the court. (See Figure 14–7.)

PHASES OF THREE–MAN PASSING GAME

A passing game offense is one in which players freelance according to predetermined guidelines governing their movements to and from various court positions. Since most movement patterns involve at most three players moving into, or operating from, scoring areas at any given time, it is possible to drill players in isolated segments of passing game offenses involving three players. (See Figures 14–8 through 14–14.)

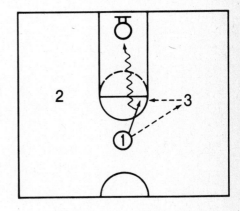

Figure 14–8 Pass and Cut Over the Top

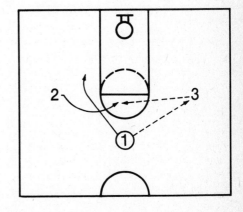

Figure 14–9 Jump Shot Over the Top

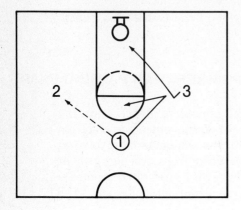

Figure 14–10   Back Cut

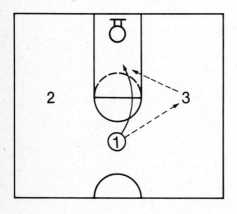

Figure 14–11   Give and Go

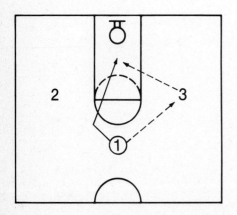

Figure 14–12   Jab and Go

Figure 14–13 Screen and Go

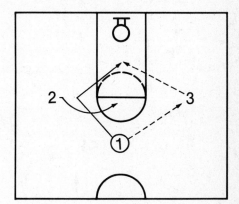

Figure 14–14 One-on-One

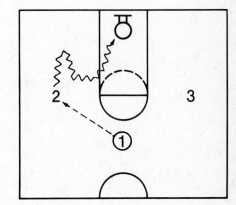

15

Power Game Offensive Breakdown Drills

In simplest terms, a *power game offense* is one that features the offensive team's attempting to create, and then exploit, one-on-one matchups inside. I love power game offenses. When I was at Long Beach State, I used power game or moving game offenses almost exclusively whenever we didn't fast break. We had a 6′6″ guard, Ed Ratleff, and I'd post him down low against smaller guards in man-to-man defenses practically every time we came crosscourt.

Sometimes, however, we had to resort to contingency patterns whenever our power offense failed. We drilled the players extensively in what to do when the basic patterns broke down.*

DRILL FOR WING ENTRY AND POST PLAY

Run the drill to O3's side one time and to O2's side the next time. (See Figures 15–1 and 15–2.) This drill can be extended to incorporate the weak-side wing into the split after the post pass. (See Figure 15–3.) Here the emphasis is on: (1) post pass and moves by O5, (2) O3 clearing to pick for O2, and (3) O2 coming off the pick for a good jump shot. Run this on both sides of the court. (See Figure 15–4.)

* For a more detailed description of Coach Tarkanian's power game offense, see *Winning Basketball Systems* (Boston: Allyn and Bacon, Inc., 1981).

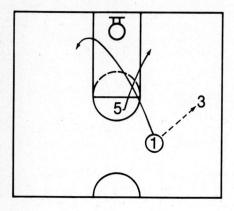

Figure 15-1   Wing Entry and
Post Play (*a*)

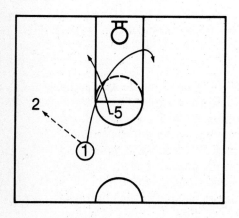

Figure 15-2   Wing Entry and
Post Play (*b*)

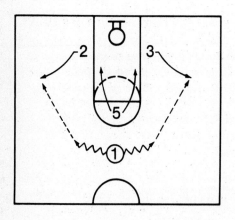

Figure 15-3   Wing Entry and
Post Play (*c*)

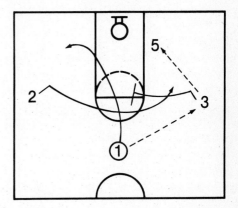

Figure 15–4   Wing Entry and
Post Play (*d*)

REVERSAL DRILLS FOR O1, O2, AND O3

If ball goes back to strong side: (1) shot or post pass by O1, and (2) reverse to O2 at free-throw line. (See Figure 15–5.)

If ball reverses sides of the floor, the emphasis is on: (1) O3 posting up, (2) pass to post by O2, and (3) drive by O2. (See Figure 15–6.)

In the reversal from O2's side, the emphasis is on: (1) pick by O3 on O1, (2) quick shot or drive by O1, (3) O3 picking for O2, (4) baseline shot or drive by O2, and (5) O3 posting up. (See Figure 15–7.)

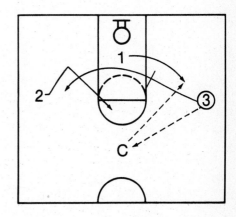

Figure 15–5   Reversal Drills for
O1, O2, and O3 (*a*)

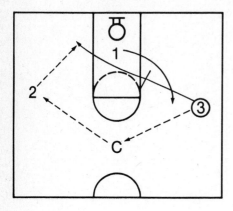

Figure 15–6 Reversal Drills for
O1, O2, and O3 (*b*)

REVERSAL DRILLS FOR O4 AND O5

In the reversal from O2's side, the emphasis is on: (1) quick dribble
rub by O4, and (2) O4 rubbing off O5 for pass over the top. (See
Figure 15–8.) In Figure 15–9, the emphasis is on: (1) pass to O5 at
the free-throw line, and (2) shot by O5 or dump to O4. In Figure
15–10 the emphasis is on: (1) post positioning, and (2) weak-side
board by O4. In Figure 15–11, the emphasis is on: (1) pick away by
O4, and (2) board play by O4 and O5.

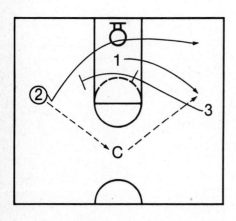

Figure 15–7 Reversal Drills for
O1, O2, and O3 (*c*)

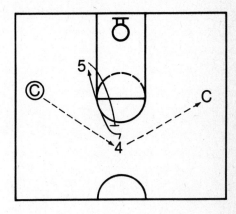

Figure 15–8 Reversal Drills for
O4 and O5 (*a*)

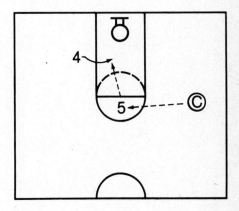

Figure 15–9 Reversal Drills for
O4 and O5 (*b*)

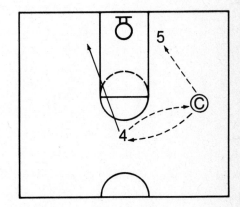

Figure 15–10 Reversal Drills
for O4 and O5 (*c*)

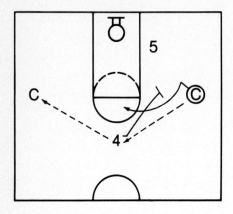

Figure 15–11   Reversal Drills for O4 and O5 (*d*)

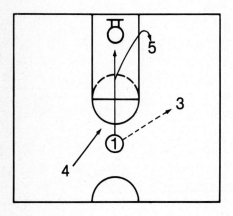

Figure 15–12   Reversal from O3's Side (*a*)

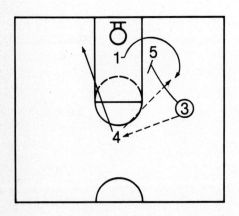

Figure 15–13   Reversal from O3's Side (*b*)

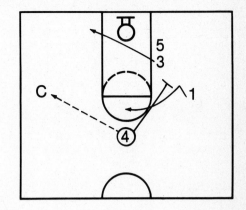

Figure 15–14 Reversal from
O3's Side (c)

REVERSAL PASS FROM O3's SIDE (FOUR-MAN DRILL)

Here the emphasis is on: (1) quick drive by O4, (2) shot by O1 off
pick, and (3) post pass by O1 to O5. (See Figures 15–12 and 15–13.)
In the complete floor reversal, the emphasis is on: (1) O3 posting
up, and (2) O4 picking away. (See Figure 15–14.)

REVERSAL PASS FROM O2's SIDE (FOUR-MAN DRILL)

Here the emphasis is on: (1) reversal pass, (2) O4 on dribble rub,
(3) O1 hitting post, (4) O2 passing to O4 over the top, and (5) O2 for
shot or drive off baseline. (See Figures 15–15 and 15–16.)

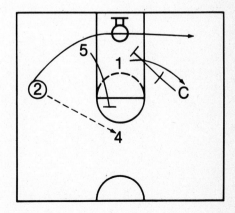

Figure 15–15 Reversal from
O2's Side (a)

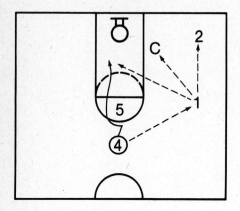

Figure 15–16   Reversal from O2's Side (*b*)

16

Pressure Man-to-Man Defensive Drills

In teaching any system of man-to-man defense, it is important to start at the most basic level—that is, with one-on-one drills featuring a single defender and a single offensive player. In teaching on-the-ball defense, all you have to do is give one player the ball, tell the defender how you want him to guard his man, and have them practice the drill. We use the Z drill (see Chapter 11) on a split-court basis, with two men on either side of the court, one working his way downcourt with the ball, and the other dogging him, attempting to draw charging fouls, forcing him one way and then the other, and trying to control his forward progress. We put guards and small forwards on one side of the court in pairs and tall forwards and centers on the other side of the court and work them mercilessly on this drill.

In teaching off-the-ball defense, the coach (or a manager, or another player) stands in one area with the ball in a ready position while one offensive player tries to elude his defender so as to receive a pass. Meanwhile, the defender uses whatever defensive techniques his coach is stressing in covering his man or denying the pass.

From one-on-one drills, we progress to two-on-two drills, including combating screens. We use guard-guard drills, guard-forward drills, guard-pivot drills, and forward-pivot drills, to accustom our players to reacting to various ball and court positions.

After two-on-two drills, we move to three-on-three drills, including screening away from the ball and splitting the post. Four-on-four drills are next, although we go back to earlier three-on-three, two-on-two, or one-on-one drills if we find that the players aren't prepared for four-on-four drills.

In our favorite four-on-four drill, the offensive team must bring the ball down against a full-court defense and pass it first to one coach stationed out of bounds on one side of the court and then to another coach located out of bounds on the other side of the court before it tries to score. Meanwhile, the defense denies the dribble toward the sidelines (which, although differing greatly from our sideline influence style, still permits practice in controlling the dribbler's movements), and plays the passing lanes so as to deny passes from the coaches back inbounds. A tremendous physical effort on the part of the defenders is required to make this drill work. However, the forty-five seconds or thereabouts that it takes the offensive team to work the ball downcourt, pass to each sideline, and then work for their shot gets our kids in shape to play tough defense for prolonged periods.

For our five-on-five drills, we use a technique known as controlled scrimmaging, in which five defenders use our sideline-influence techniques until either the offense scores (in which case, the ball is brought back out and the sequence begins again, with the same teams on offense and defense) or the defense steals the ball or claims a defensive rebound and fast breaks. If the defenders miss their shot, they press the offensive team full court.

Our controlled scrimmaging gives our players intensified practice in two phases of the game, half-court pressure man-to-man defensive techniques and fast breaking. We practice other phases of the game, of course, but not from *this* type of controlled scrimmaging. The players must concentrate on what they're doing, and we don't think they can concentrate on beating the press, running a half-court offense, and using bringin plays and tipoff plays, in addition to all the drills we emphasize in our controlled scrimmaging. They'll have to demonstrate all these tactics in games, of course, but we want them to learn the many defensive skills they'll have to perform in small doses. We'd stress defense alone, except that our offense *is* our transition game. If we don't fast break and get into our quick-shot offense, we don't play effectively.*

Before discussing other man-to-man drills, we might mention a simple three-on-three drill designed to increase players' aggres-

* For a detailed analysis of our man-to-man defensive philosophy, techniques and drills, see *Winning Basketball Systems* (Boston: Allyn and Bacon, Inc., 1981).

siveness. It can be used effectively in any coaching situation, regardless of the players' skills and the extent of the coach's involvement. The drill does not rely on coaching involvement for its effectiveness, since it is self-motivating.

All the players line up in three lines at half court. The first player in each line turns around to face the next player in his line, and those six players go three-on-three. If the offensive team scores, the defensive team runs the bleachers five times (or runs a specified number of laps or step-slides across the court and back). If an offensive player makes a layup, the penalty may be increased to, say, *seven* bleachers in order to illustrate the point that "we don't allow layups around here." If a defender commits a foul, he runs three bleachers and is replaced by the next player in his line.

If the defense steals the ball or forces a turnover before the offensive team takes a shot, the *offensive* players must run three bleachers before taking their place on defense. (In fact, the only time that nobody has to run bleachers occurs when the offensive team shoots and misses and the defensive team gets the rebound.) If the offensive team shoots and gets the rebound, play continues as before until either the defense gets the ball back or the offense scores.

When the offensive team scores or the defensive team gets the ball, play stops, and the next three players in line become the next three offensive players. The offensive players move to defense (provided they don't have to run bleachers for failing to get a shot), and the defenders move to the back of the line at half court (provided they also don't have to run bleachers). Any time players have to run bleachers, they go to the end of the line at half court when they're finished. When offensive players have to run bleachers, the defensive players stay out on the court while the next three players in line go on offense.

This kind of drill is excellent for those practices in which nothing seems to go right, and you must find a way to get players back on track. If the players don't hustle and concentrate after running a series of bleachers, no other tactic is likely to work, either, except perhaps running drills.

DEFENSING THE BALLHANDLER COMING UP THE FLOOR

1. Influence the ballhandler toward the outside of the court, giving him only one direction to go.

2. After the ballhandler begins moving in the desired direction, square up and apply pressure.

3. Drive him to the sideline, using it as a cutoff point (top of the circle extended on the hash mark).

4. Do not allow him to reverse from the sideline and drive the middle.

5. If he gets away along the sideline, use the baseline as a cutoff point.

6. When he gives the ball up, deny the quick inside cut and seek proper position in relation to the ball and your man.

GUARD DRILLS

The primary factors to remember here are:

1. Influence, get in motion, square up, cut off, and deny dribble reversal. (See Figure 16–1.)

2. Get off and to the ball after your man passes it; help position to deny reversal. (You can also use influence and motion.) The emphasis is on having the offense post up also and defensing on pivot area by the guard. (See Figure 16–2.)

3. Two-man drill: incorporate all guard defensive techniques—influence, motion, square up, cut off, next receiver, deny reversal, get off with the pass, help defense, post defense, and jump switch crosses. Remember that you can pass to the coach and cut at any time. (See Figure 16–3.)

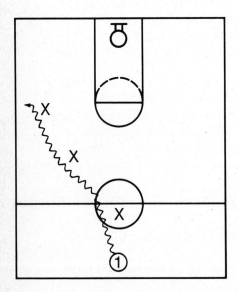

Figure 16–1   Guard Drills (*a*)

Figure 16–2 Guard Drills (*b*)

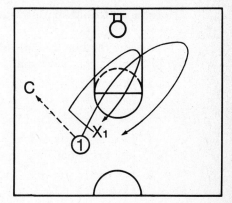

Figure 16–3 Guard Drills (*c*)

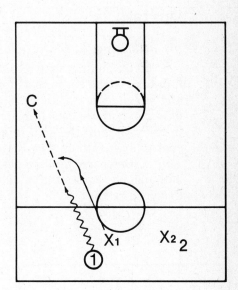

Defensing the Stationary Man With the Ball

1. Influence to the baseline.
2. Do not let him drive across the top.
3. Cutoff point is at the baseline three feet outside the free-throw lane.
4. Do not let him reverse off the baseline across the middle.

Defensing the Man Without the Ball

1. The farther the ball is from your man, the farther you slide away from your man.
2. Deny the pass if it is in the next receiver position (elbow and foot in the passing lane).
3. See your man and the ball at all times.
4. Lead all weak-side cuts to the ball, and front anything in the key area (baseline to top of circle).
5. Be ready to help in breakdown situations—protect the basket!
6. Never let your man cross in front of you.

FORWARD DRILLS

The primary factors to remember here are:

1. Defending next receiver, backdoor cut, man with the ball, influence to the baseline, cutoff point, deny drive across the middle, and one-on-one. Shoulders should be parallel to sideline when the player gets to the baseline or squared up as soon as possible. Early in the year, run the drill in a controlled environment; later in the year, play it full on. (See Figure 16–4.)

2. Defensive forward position drill: Adjust to movement of the ball, defense across the middle, and help in breakdown situations. (See Figure 16–5.)

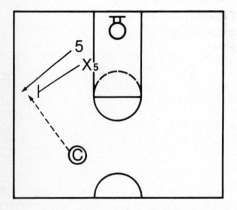

Figure 16–4 Forward Drills (a)

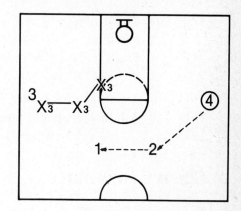

Figure 16–5 Forward Drills (*b*)

3. Two-man forward drill: Adjust to movement of the ball, defense all cuts, and play two-on-two across the middle to score. (See Figure 16–6.)

It is paramount to this defense that the ball never goes into the high- or low-post areas. If the ball is passed or dribbled into the post area, all perimeter pressure is lost.

Coaching Points

1. Front everything inside the key from the baseline to the top of the circle.

2. Front the high post—it takes away a lot of offense.

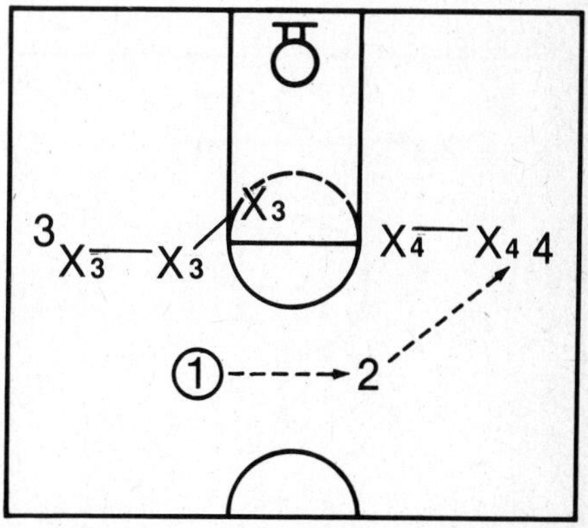

Figure 16–6 Forward Drills (*c*)

3. Try to obtain a "bottom" front in the low post whenever possible.

4. Front on ball side in high post.

5. Use the "V" technique in fronting.

6. Encourage lob passes—need weak-side help.

7. All players should know fronting techniques.

DEFENSIVE POST DRILL

1. Start offense in low post; defense reacts to ball movement; execute proper front in relationship to ball position; delay and then bring offensive post to the ball. (See Figure 16–7.)

2. Start offense in high post; react to ball movement; slide post low and play proper defense; incorporate breakdown defensive responsibilities. (See Figure 16–8.)

Entries—High to low. (See Figures 16–9 and 16–10.)

Coaching Points

1. Establish defensive set at some point above the foul line. *Do not set up deep in the lane and wait.*

2. Force post to cut behind the defender. *Do not let the cutter "across your face."*

3. Establish high front and deny the ball with ball-side elbow in the lane.

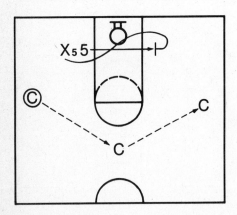

Figure 16–7   Defensive Post Drills (*a*)

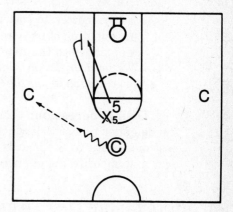

Figure 16–8   Defensive Post
Drills (*b*)

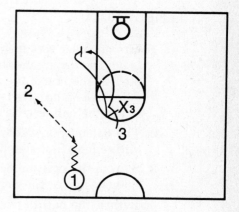

Figure 16–9   Defensive Post
Drills (*c*)

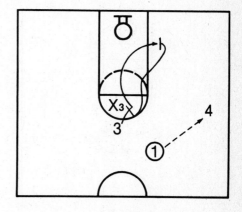

Figure 16–10   Defensive Post
Drills (*d*)

4. Escort cutter to low post and establish low-post front. In anticipation of pass from O2 back to point and the post man's stepping into the hole, *do not drop low defensive foot below the level of the post man's top foot so as to facilitate getting over the top when the ball is returned to the point.*

Drill Progression: O2 and O3 can drive the baseline, forcing the defender to a true low post front. O2 and O3 can shoot as both post men work to the boards. Defender "slips" inside if possible or over and opposite the offensive man's turn.

GUARD-TO-GUARD LINE ADJUSTMENTS

Coaching Points

In Figure 16–11:

1. The defender sets inside and above low post when the ball is outside the area of the extended free-throw line. He is one step off the line of the ball with his eyes in an "off the ball" defensive stance. He is thus in a position to deny a vertical cut to the ball or a corner-release cut.

2. The defender moves with the pass, opening up to the ball with a long first step as the post man cuts across the lane.

3. Step to the position described in the first point as the post man sets up at the completion of his cut.

4. Return the ball to O1 and repeat. Remember the defender must move with each pass. Anticipate the pass.

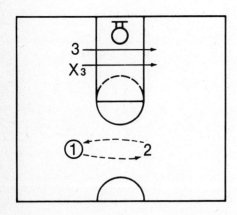

Figure 16–11   Guard-to-Guard Line Adjustment

Drill Progression: O3 cuts up the lane to the ball and back down to low post. O3 releases to the corner or wing and back to low post at the beginning or end of the drill.

LOW-POST FRONT

Coaching Points

In Figure 16–12:

1. Defender starts in low post front and reacts to ball movement. Delay offense and then bring to ball.
2. Low-post front is a "V" front with elbow in the passing lane.
3. Defender must get "over" as the ball is passed to O1—stop the post man from stepping into the hole.
4. As the offense continues the cut, the defense makes every effort to get over all the way to a low front as O3 receives the ball.
5. Also practice defender reacting to offense when he steps up into the hole and then to opposite low post.
6. Repeat the process as O3 passes to O1, and as O1 passes to O2. The defender can get from a low post front to the top more effectively by "slipping" over. Lift back arm and step with back foot "slicing" over the post man.

Drill Progression: O4 cuts all the way to O1 and touches the ball. The defender does the same. O4 then cuts to opposite low post

Figure 16–12 Low-Post Front

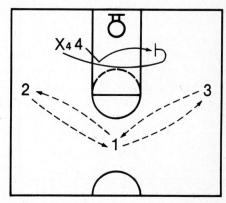

as the ball is passed to O3. The defender stays on ball side and uses a head snap if necessary.

TRIANGLE DRILL (HIGH-POST DENIAL)

Coaching Points

In Figure 16–13:

1. The defender sets up two steps from the post man and one step off the line of the ball for vision.
2. O4 cuts diagonally to a position halfway into the top of the circle and outside the lane line. The defender escorts O4, using short sliding adjustments and the "elbow in the passing lane" principle.
3. As O2 passes to O1, the defender gets over in a slip move, stepping with his back foot and lifting his back arm. He then escorts O4 across the lane, staying on ball side as the ball is passed to O3.
4. O3 drives the lane, and O4 cuts to low post as the defender escorts him down the lane and establishes a low front. Stay over the top, if possible. As the ball is passed from O1 to O3, the defender may get caught behind O4. If so, beat him low and establish a low front. Remember that the defender can't get to the cutoff mark if he is caught behind low post on ball side.

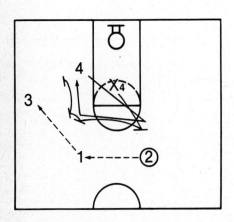

Figure 16–13   Triangle Drill

Drill Progression: The defender cuts off as O3 drives the baseline.

GUARD-TO-FORWARD (HIGH POST)

Coaching Points

In Figure 16–14:

1. When O1 passes to O2, an adustment is necessary. If the defender goes "over," the offense will get him on his back and take the lead pass for a layup.
2. The adjustment should be made behind the offensive center with a quick change in position to prevent the post man from dropping low.
3. Establish position to block and hold as high as possible. Step with the high foot and with the low foot as the ball is passed.

Drill Progression: After the defender establishes the ball-side set, O3 cuts away low and back to ball-side low post. The defender does not follow O3 away but establishes line of the ball defense, escorts O3 across the lane, and establishes a low-post front. O2 can drive baseline, with the defender cutting him off.

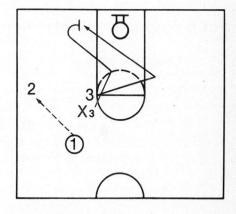

Figure 16–14 Guard-to-Forward (High-Post) Drill

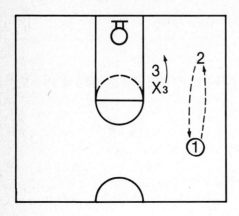

Figure 16–15 Medium-Post Reaction

MEDIUM-POST REACTION

Coaching Points

In Figure 16–15:

1. Establish inside post position, with O1 with the ball. The ball is passed back and forth, with the receiver holding the ball for two seconds.
2. The defender gets over the top whenever possible. Go behind as a last resort. The defender will not be able to get to the cutoff point if caught behind the post man.

   Drill Progression: O2 drives, and the defender cuts him off.

FOUR CORNERS (MULTIPURPOSE DRILL)

Coaching Points

In Figure 16–16:

1. O1 has the ball. The defender maintains his defensive line as the ball is passed to O3. O5 cuts to the ball as the defender escorts him through the lane and then establishes a low front.
2. O3 returns the ball to O1, and O5 cuts to high post. The defender maintains position with his elbow in the lane.

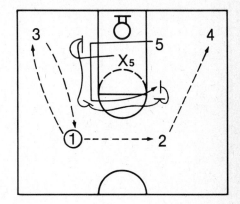

Figure 16–16 Four-Corners Multipurpose Drill (*a*)

3. O1 passes to O2 as O5 cuts across, and the defender goes over the top to high post.

4. O2 hits O4 and O5 goes down the lane, with the defender using snap-around in getting to low front. Anticipate and move with every pass. Take initiative in getting over the top.

Drill Progression: Call "lob" any time the ball is at O3 or O4, and defense with a long step and jump.

HIGH-POST RELEASE (DENIAL)

Coaching Points

In Figure 16–17:

1. O1 and O2 set up outside the midcourt line and pass the ball back and forth, with the defender adjusting his line.

2. The coach calls "Go!" O3 cuts to the ball. The defender plays lead denial all the way to the ball. Both O3 and the defender touch the ball. The defender must adjust his defensive split in accordance with the distance between the ball and high post.

Drill Progression: The defender must have the experience of stealing the ball and driving for a layup.

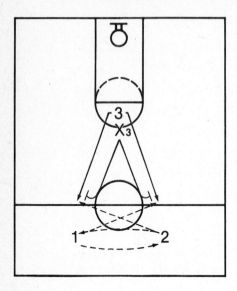

Figure 16–17 High-Post Release Drill

TEAM AND BREAKDOWN DEFENSE

Breakdown defense refers to the defensive team's efforts to restore normalcy to the situation, that is, to regain defensive control when the offensive team has been able to thwart the defense's strategy, whether by driving the middle other than along the baseline, passing inside to a post man, or passing to a cutter going backdoor. In such a situation, when the defense has "broken down," emergency measures are clearly indicated.

Team defense is played with the following basic rules:

1. Constantly strive to find the proper defensive position in relation to the ball and your man, always adjusting your position.
2. Never allow an offensive player to penetrate between you and your defensive partner.
3. The farther away the ball, the farther you move away from your man. The closer the ball, the closer you get to your man.
4. In breakdown situations—those in which a defensive man is beaten—all five players must react promptly and properly.

Team Defense Drill

Four-on-four drill: The offense is stationary to begin with; pass the ball slowly; the defense makes proper adjustments; put in weak-side

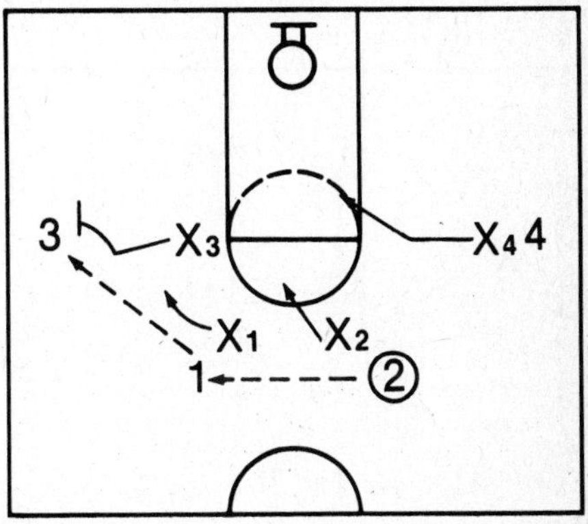

Figure 16–18 Team Defense (Breakdown) Drill (*a*)

cutters to the ball; have breakdown situations; then play live to score. (See Figures 16–18 and 16–19.)

FULL-COURT DOUBLE TEAMS AND ROTATION GUARD DRILLS

Coaching Points

1. Practice both letting them get the ball in-bounds and denying the passes. In the former case, influence the receivers toward predetermined areas of the court. (See Figure 16–20.)

2. Pick up the opponents with tough head-up man-to-man pressure defense once the ball is inbounded. (See Figure 16–21.)

3. Try to keep the dribbler to the outside of the court.

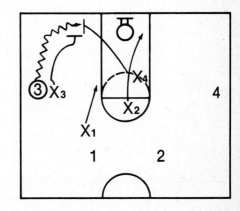

Figure 16–19 Team Defense (Breakdown) Drill (*b*)

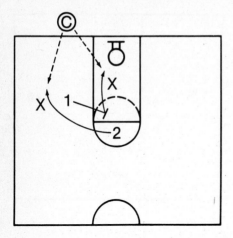

Figure 16–20 Full-Court Double Teams and Rotation Guard Drills (*a*)

4. Square up and cut the dribbler off on the sideline, thus forcing him to spin-dribble off the sideline or pick the ball up.

5. Have the defensive guard on weak side point his man and the ball (that is, point one hand at the dribbler and the other hand at his man), using bluffs and fakes toward the ball if the dribbler comes at him. If the dribbler turns his back, spin dribbles or picks the ball, the weak-side guard will double-team. (See Figure 16–22.)

6. If the ball is passed over the double team into the middle of the court, have the guard on the ball pick up the closest forward on his side of the court.

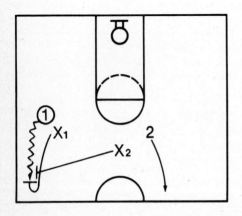

Figure 16–21 Full-Court Double Teams and Rotation Guard Drills (*b*)

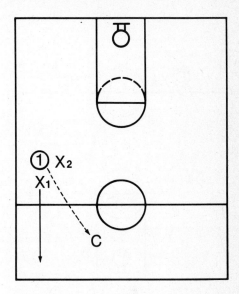

Figure 16–22 Full-Court Double Teams and Rotation Guard Drills (*c*)

FORWARD-CENTER DRILLS

Coaching Points

1. Get a proper split between your man and the ball as it advances downcourt. (See Figure 16–23.)

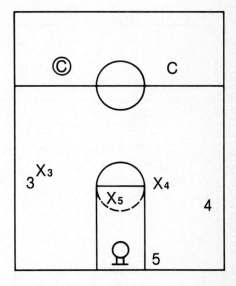

Figure 16–23 Forward-Center Drills (*a*)

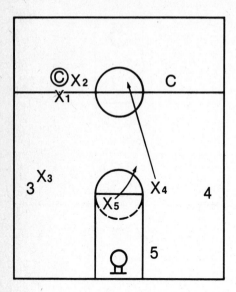

Figure 16–24 Forward-Center
Drills (*b*)

2. Try to discern when the defensive guards are going to double team. Otherwise, the trap will be sprung, but the passing lanes will still be open. (See Figure 16–24.)

3. When double teaming occurs: (a) the weak-side forward takes away the guard-to-guard pass; (b) the ball-side forward covers the middle; and (c) the center covers the deep zone. (See Figure 16–25.)

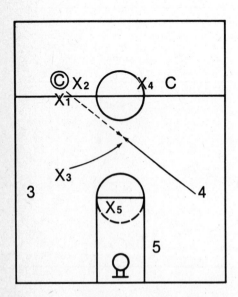

Figure 16–25 Forward-Center
Drills (*c*)

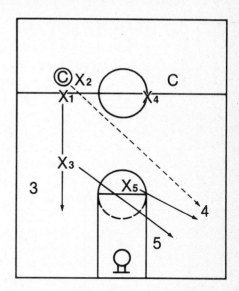

Figure 16–26   Forward-Center Drills (*d*)

4. If a pass is completed into the middle, the ball side forward covers the pass receiver. (See Figure 16–25.)

5. If a pass is completed all the way across the court out of the double team: (a) the center covers the pass receiver; and (b) the ball-side forward covers the post. (See Figure 16–26.)

COMBINATION DRILL

Coaching Point

Put the guards and back-line players together and drill the various possibilities of offensive movement. The defense must react to: (a) initial pressure and double teaming by the guards; (b) proper rotation on the double team by players farthest away from the ball; and (c) rotation if the pass penetrates the middle or to the deep corner out of the double team. (See Figure 16–27.)

CONTROLLED SCRIMMAGING

In the previous section, we described a number of situational drills designed to familiarize defensive players with their responsibilities for assuming various ball positions and player combinations—for example, a single defender at the point influencing the dribbler toward the sideline, a guard and forward covering their men, two

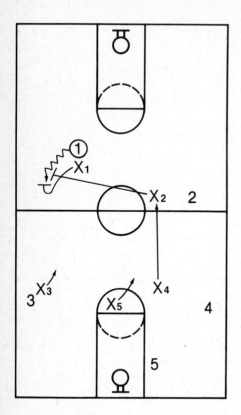

Figure 16–27   Combination Drill

defensive guards (or a guard and a forward) and a defensive forward placed against three offensive players, or four defenders covering two guards and two forwards (or a forward and a center). Though these drills are vital to the learning process in teaching man-to-man defense, we feel that it is also necessary to simulate game conditions if players are to overcome their confusion about how the techniques are actually deployed in games.

To be most effective, we see that scrimmaging must be arranged into tightly structured sequences that emphasize one or two specific skills as opposed to having players work on jump-ball situations, baseline and sideline bringins, offensive patterns, free throws, pressing defense, half-court coverage, and the transition game within the context of a single scrimmage, or drill. A team cannot learn to play man-to-man defense effectively while running offensive patterns, and in scrimmaging full-court players tend to lose their concentration rather easily. We use full-court scrimmaging, but we *always* do it within the context of man-to-man defense and the transition game.

Perhaps the best way to show the difference between drills, scrimmaging, and controlled scrimmaging is to imagine a given team on the court with the ball. Let's say the players intend to work on their zone offense. In drilling, they would get the ball back after scores, turnovers, or defensive rebounds in order to practice their half-court zone offense as much as possible. In full-court scrimmaging, they would work on their zone offensive patterns only when they had the ball at their end of the court. In controlled scrimmaging, they would start every sequence with the ball at their end of the court and would also get the ball back after scores to start a new sequence. However, they would also be expected to work on getting back quickly on defense after turnovers and defensive rebounds. (Of course, after the players retreated and stopped the opponents' fast break, they would start another sequence with the ball at that end of the court.)

Although it is possible to use controlled scrimmaging in combinations, we prefer either four-on-four or five-on-five situations. (In practicing zone defense, we used to play five defenders against as many as seven or eight players.) In four-on-four or five-on-five situations, we practice on-the-ball defense, coverage one pass away from the ball, and weak-side coverage and post coverage at the same time. In short, we can bring into play all the elements in defensive coverage, and when transitions occur, we can fill *four* lanes in fast breaking. Of course, by the time our controlled scrimmaging is begun, we've worked our players through one-on-one, two-on-two and three-on-three drills. Whenever breakdowns arise in our basic coverage, we go back to those drills to work out the problems.

Defensively, controlled scrimmaging is generally (but not always) used to practice defense and the transition game. In addition to half-court defense and fast breaking after turnovers, we use controlled scrimmaging to practice our full-court defense. We either start with players already in position or on offense with a shot having been taken and made (to get the players accustomed to finding their men quickly after scores).

In terms of coverage, we may either go straight man-to-man or leave the inbounds passer unguarded and double team one of the other offensive players, depending upon our defensive strategy.* When the defense steals the ball, it fast breaks and goes into its early offense. As a result, the sequences provide ample practice in three phrases of the game: our half-court defense (or full-court defense), anticipating turnovers, and fast breaking after turnovers.

* For a detailed analysis of full-court pressing techniques, see our book *Winning Basketball Systems* (Boston: Allyn and Bacon, Inc., 1981).

In a typical controlled scrimmaging sequence (working on full-court pressure man-to-man defense), we have the offensive team inbound the ball and attempt to bring it to their end of the court. If the players are able to accomplish this, we station coaches out of bounds on either side of the court at the offensive end. Before the offensive players are allowed to shoot, they must pass the ball first to one coach, and then to the other, with the defenders attempting to deny the passes back inbounds. It usually takes about forty-five seconds for the offensive team to bring the ball downcourt, pass to both coaches, and work for a good shot. (If the offense is able to accomplish these tasks in considerably less time on a consistent basis, the defenders are not applying themselves as arduously as they might.) This sequence teaches players to concentrate and play tough defense for extended periods of time, and as a result, to increase their mental toughness. It is also ideal for teaching players to anticipate transitions, and as a result, to become involved in fast breaking when they might not otherwise. The success of any fast break is determined in the two to three seconds before and after transitions occur. If, through practice, repetition and drill, a player becomes one and one-half steps faster than he was previously in recognizing and reacting to transitions, he will be more likely to take advantage of the situation than players who do not work on transitional phases of the game.

When we aren't particularly interested in working on our full-court press, we use a four-on-four drill on a half-court basis, fast breaking after steals and defensive rebounds, with the offense keeping the ball after scores and offensive rebounds. This drill is, for all practical purposes, our multipurpose team drill, since we can practice everything from on-the-ball, weak-side, and post coverage to breakdown automatics (automatic movements by teammates necessary to restore a semblance of normalcy to the defensive coverage when it "breaks down"). The four positions used in four-on-four drills may be varied by using either two guards and two forwards, two guards, a forward and a center, or one guard, two forwards, and a center. As before, the defenders will fast break on steals and defensive rebounds. (If they shoot at the end of the fast break, we allow them to take a second or third shot, but not to take the ball back outside and set up.)

17

Zone Defensive
Drills

1-2-2 (HELP-AND-RECOVER) ZONE DEFENSIVE DRILLS

Baseline Corner Drill

The three offensive men remain stationary and pass the ball quickly. The two defenders must not allow a shot out of their respective corners and must move together as if attached by an invisible rope like two mountain climbers. (See Figures 17-1 and 17-2.)

> **Note:** When the ball is returned to the point, the defenders return to their starting positions. To stop the corner shot, players should run in a crouched position, if running is necessary to get them in good defensive position to deny the shot. The rest of their movements should consist of quick pivots, shuffling, and sliding. When attacking the man in the corner, players must favor his baseline side.

Point-Wing Drill

Two offensive men attack point X1, who must get help from his teammates at the defensive wings to deny the outside shot. The wing men advance with their inside foot forward and retreat by dropping that inside foot and shuffling. (See Figure 17-3.)

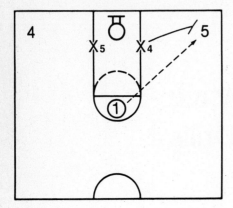

Figure 17–1   Baseline Corner Drill (*a*)

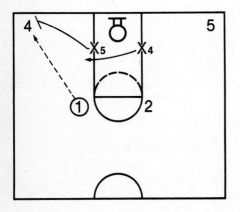

Figure 17–2   Baseline Corner Drill (*b*)

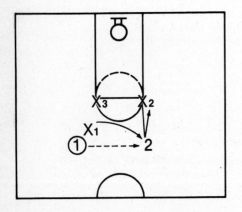

Figure 17–3   Point-Wing Drill

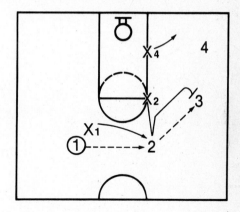

Figure 17–4   Point-Wing-Baseline Drill (*a*)

Note: The point guard defends the ball. When the ball is passed to O2, X1 must chase the ball. Wing X2 advances and contests the ball until X1 arrives—usually, no more than a second after X2 assumes momentary coverage. X2 then retreats to his starting point and anticipates a pass to the post.

Point-Wing-Baseline Drill

The four offensive men move the ball, with the three ball-side men looking for the shot. The three defenders must move together and deny every shot attempted. This is a very difficult drill for the wing men. The baseline and wing men prevent post passes. (See Figures 17–4 and 17–5.)

Note: If O1 has the ball, he is defended by X1. When O1 passes to O2, X2 comes up and defends until X1 gets to the ball. When

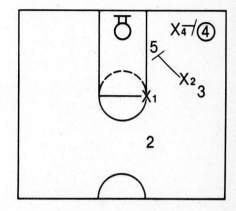

Figure 17–5   Point-Wing-Baseline Drill (*b*)

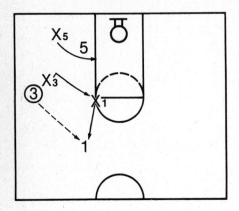

Figure 17–6 Drill for Denying the Post Pass

O2 passes to O3, the wing man must stop the shot. When O3 passes to O4, X4 must stop the shot, and X2 sags down to deny the post pass.

Drill for Denying the Post Pass

Note: The wing man (X3) pivots quickly to intercept the guard-to-post pass. The wing men play with their arms out to the sides and try to steal as many passes as possible. They should be encouraged to jump into the passing lanes on occasion. If wing men are in the passing lanes, the back-line defenders move up one step to cover open areas. (See Figure 17–6.)

Seven-On-Five Drill

Now the five defenders can work together against the offense's numerical superiority. No shots are to be allowed. The offensive post

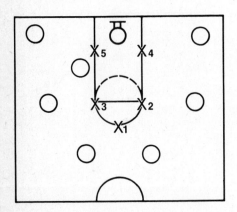

Figure 17–7 Seven-on-Five Drill

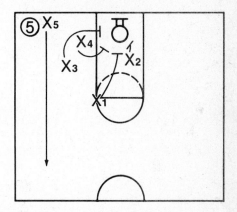

Figure 17–8 Rebounding Drill
(*a*)

man may move anywhere he likes inside the zone. He can even break the three-second rule inside the lane. Outside offensive players are encouraged to pass quickly, to attempt to split a seam, and to penetrate or drive the baseline. (See Figure 17–7.)

> **Note:** If an offensive player penetrates and receives the ball, he should be trapped. The ball must not be allowed inside. If the offensive team passes inside, the defensive players collapse on the offensive players with their hands up to encourage a slow pass (lob or bounce) back outside.

Rebounding Drill

In Figures 17–8 through 17–10, the defender covering the shooter releases downcourt to facilitate the ensuing fast break. Many coaches prefer not to release anyone early, particularly if the opponents excel in offensive rebounding. We don't release in our pressure man-to-man defense at UNLV.

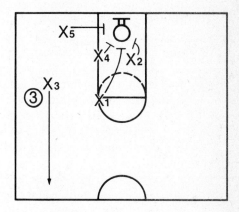

Figure 17–9 Rebounding Drill
(*b*)

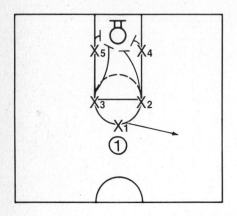

Figure 17–10   Rebounding Drill
(*c*)

SUMMARY

All movement in the 1–2–2 zone defense is accomplished in basic
man-to-man fashion, that is, knees bent, head up, back straight,
and feet wider apart than the shoulders and ready to move. The
baseline men may have to sprint to the corners to deny shots. If so,
they must sprint from a crouched position and attack *from the baseline side of the offensive player.* All movement, with this single exception, constitutes the basic shuffle and slide step.

Players must work hard. They can never afford to relax when
the ball is not in their area of responsibility.

Players must never concede the pass inside. They should try
not to allow the ball inside to a low-post position or to high post.

All players must move quickly and as a unit to defend the ball.

After the offense has established its passing lanes along the
perimeters of the defense, the defenders may gamble and play the
passing lanes. They must do this quickly and with recovery in mind
in case the steal or deflection attempt is unsuccessful. The fundamentals involved in the breakdown drills should be mastered before
going on to the five-man defense.

In the course of the season, less and less time will be necessary
to keep players sharp in this defense. If at times the defense is not
being played as well as expected, the coach can always return to the
breakdown drills and start over.

Players will gain a tremendous psychological edge when playing seven-on-five and being able to stop the offense from getting a
decent shot.

Rebounding responsibilities as diagrammed should be under-
stood by everyone. If players get burned on long rebounds, the coach

should eliminate early releases downcourt by any of the defenders. The ball is more important than an open-man downcourt.

The defense's goal is to deny any kind of inside game, while the players sharply limit the opponents' outside shots. No aspect of the opponents' offense should be conceded; every offensive movement must be countered. If even one man fails to fulfill his defensive responsibilities, the 1–2–2 defense will not be effective.

2–1–2 ZONE DEFENSIVE DRILLS

Help-and-Recover Drill

This is the most important drill in teaching effective 2–1–2 zone defense. Help and recover is the order of the day in this drill. The baseline defender comes up quickly, denies any shot, and stops any penetration until the outside man on his side can get over and release him to cover the now vulnerable area at low post. (See Figure 17–11.)

> **Note:** O1 is defended by outside defender X1. O1 passes to O2, who is picked up by baseline defender X5. X5 must not allow the shot, and he must stop any penetration by O2. When X1 arrives and assumes good defensive position on the ball, X5 releases and picks up O3. X5 must be wary of the penetrating pass to the area he has vacated close to the basket.
>
> During a game, high-post defender X3 would slide down and cover the ball side low post.

Figure 17–11 Help-and-Recover Drill

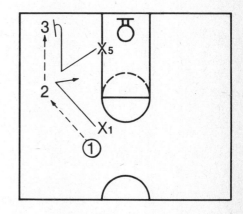

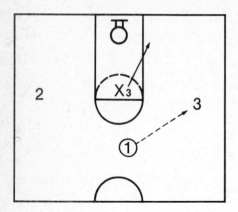

Figure 17–12   Post-Man Drill

Post Drill

The three offensive players pass the ball quickly, forcing the post defender to move. The coach can put in a high-post offensive player and make the post defender fight around him in order to maintain proper defensive positioning. (See Figure 17–12.)

Six-on-Five Drill

The offensive players should be encouraged to pass the ball quickly. Help-and-recover must be effective or the offense will have a field day picking the defense apart. (See Figure 17–13.)

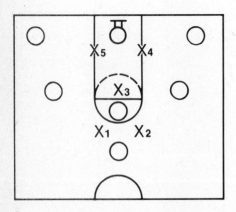

Figure 17–13   Six-on-Five Drill

SUMMARY

Players must work hard. As in the 1–2–2 drills, players can never afford to relax when the ball is not in their area.

The areas at the extended free-throw line are vulnerable, and the baseline man on ball side must guard the ball in that area until the outside defender on his side can hustle over and release him. The help-and-recover drill and the six-on-five drill are very important in teaching players to move quickly and react to rapid ball and player movements in zone offenses.

X1 and X2 can guide the ball to a particular area of the court if one of them plays the ball head up. At times, they may encourage a penetrating move and then trap the offensive player with the ball.

X1 and X2 must be able to protect the point, wings and high-post areas. Though they will get momentary help at the wings from the baseline defenders on their respective sides, they must move quickly to release that defender to cover the corner or low post.

X3 must defend the high post, rebound, and help eliminate low-post play. He must be wary of allowing the high-post offensive to turn and face the basket with the ball.

If the ball gets inside somehow, everyone collapses with their hands up to force a slow pass (lob or bounce) back outside.

1-3-1 ZONE DEFENSIVE TRAPPING DRILLS

Sprint-Slide Drill

Deep defender X5 must start at least fifteen feet from the man in the corner. When the pass is made to the offensive man in the corner,

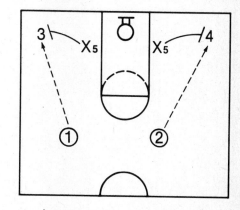

Figure 17–14 Sprint-Slide Drill

the defender must sprint at the man with the ball, favoring the baseline. When he is within six feet of the man, the defender must slide up to him with a hand up so the offensive player cannot pass over the man or dribble around him. He must stop the man in a one-on-one situation.

This drill is excellent for use with any zone defense. (See Figure 17–14.)

Sprint-Slide Drill (Variation)

The defender does the same as in the previous drill except that, on the pass, he sprints forward until he is six feet away from his man and then slides up to him with hand raised and inside foot forward. (See Figure 17–15.)

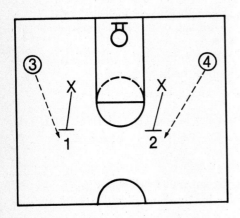

Figure 17–15 Sprint-Slide Drill (Variation)

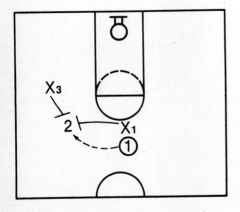

Figure 17–16 Trapping Drill

Trapping Drill

The defenders should advance on the ball quickly with their hands raised. They should not permit themselves to be split on the dribble, to allow a pass toward the basket or to allow the ballhandler to dribble out of the trap. If the ball is returned to the point, X1 must follow the ball and play tough man-to-man defense. Every player should do this drill, regardless of his position in the 1–3–1 alignment. (See Figure 17–16.)

High-Post Trap Drill

As the pass is made to the high post, X4 contains the post man, and X1 collapses to harass him. Both defenders' hands should be up to encourage the "slow" pass (either a bounce or lob pass). If the high-post man is allowed to pivot and face the basket, the entire defense is in trouble, since the high-post man is now in position to pass the ball inside or under the basket. The defenders should harass him enough to make him pass the ball back outside. If the post man dribbles, the high-post man should steal the ball from him. (See Figure 17–17.)

Six-on-Five Drill

The six offensive men will attempt to (1) delay the game, and (2) score on a good percentage shot. The defenders must harass the ballhandlers and force errors without giving up a good shot. The offense may back the ball out to half court to delay, and the defense must go out after them. (See Figure 17–18.)

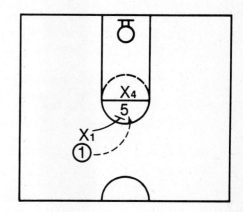

Figure 17–17 High-Post Trap Drill

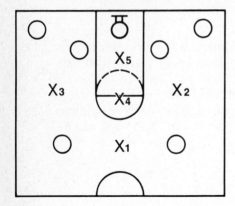

Figure 17–18   Six-on-Five Drill

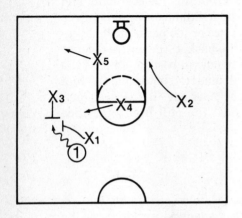

Figure 17–19   1–3–1 Trap Drill
(a)

1–3–1 Trap Drill (Extended)

The coverage is the same as in the nonextended trapping position. The defensive team is now relying on great effort from each man, anticipation by defenders away from the ball, and elimination of the high-post man by X4 in the middle. (See Figure 17–19.)

> **Note:** The ball-side wing man (X3) advances to trap as the dribbler makes his move. X1 is playing tough man-to-man defense and forcing the dribbler to the sideline. X3 must not allow the dribbler to escape him along the sideline. The high-post man is eliminated, and X2 is anticipating passes as is X5 along the baseline. (See Figure 17–20.)

> **Note:** As the ball is passed from guard to guard, wing man X3 returns to his spot on weak side, anticipating a pass over the

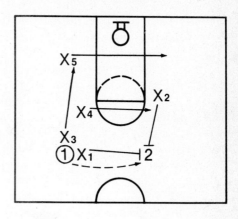

Figure 17–20 1–3–1 Trap Drill
(*b*)

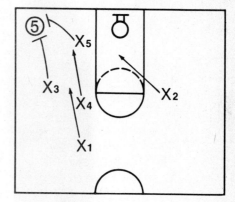

Figure 17–21 1–3–1 Trap Drill
(*c*)

defense; wing X2 attacks the guard and does not allow him to escape down the sideline; X1 hustles over to trap O2; X4 moves with the ball, favoring ball side and concentrating on eliminating the high-post pass; and X5 slides over to ball side, anticipating a pass to the corner or to the area he just vacated.

If the offense penetrates, the defenders must retreat quickly, with their hands up to encourage a lob pass back outside. (See Figure 17–21.)

SUMMARY

Start the defense in tight and extend it as necessary to harass the ball constantly.

If the ball leaves a player's area, he cannot relax but must move to his assigned position and anticipate passes or be prepared to double team.

When the defenders are trapping, they must not allow the dribbler to split them on the dribble. They must stop the dribbler. The wing men cannot allow the dribbler to escape along the sidelines.

Point guard X1, using sound man-to-man principles, must not allow a dribbler to penetrate the defense, particularly in the course of ball rotation from one side of the court to the other.

The high-post defender (X4) must eliminate the opponents' high-post attack. If he does not accomplish this, his team will have little success with the defense.

The defenders should influence the ball into seams, then stop the penetration, and trap the ballhandler. Defenders should trap with their hands up to encourage a slow pass (bounce or lob).

When the ball is in the corner, trapping possibilities are excellent (and passing lanes away from the corner are reduced).

In executing a trap, the two trapping defenders should keep their hands at ball level at all times. They are not trying to take the ball away from the offensive player necessarily, but are making it difficult for him to advance the ball. The trapping players' feet should be placed so that the offensive player will find it impossible to dribble between them. If the ballhandler has given up his dribble, the player's hands may be held high to encourage only the slow pass (bounce or lob).